Designing for Gesture and Tangible Interaction

Synthesis Lectures on Human-Centered Informatics

Editor
John M. Carroll, *Penn State University*

Human-Centered Informatics (HCI) is the intersection of the cultural, the social, the cognitive, and the aesthetic with computing and information technology. It encompasses a huge range of issues, theories, technologies, designs, tools, environments, and human experiences in knowledge work, recreation and leisure activity, teaching and learning, and the potpourri of everyday life. The series publishes state-of-the-art syntheses, case studies, and tutorials in key areas. It shares the focus of leading international conferences in HCI.

Designing for Gesture and Tangible Interaction
Mary Lou Maher and Lina Lee
March 2017

From Tool to Partner: The Evolution of Human-Computer Interaction
Jonathan Grudin
December 2016

Qualitative HCI Research: Going behind the Scenes
Ann Blandford, Dominic Furniss, and Stephann Makri
April 2016

Learner-Centered Design of Computing Education: Research on Computing for Everyone
Mark Guzdial
November 2015

The Envisionment and Discovery Collaboratory (EDC): Explorations in Human-Centered Informatics with Tabletop Computing Environments
Ernesto G. Arias, Hal Eden, and Gerhard Fischer
October 2015

Humanistic HCI
Jeffrey Bardzell and Shaowen Bardzell
September 2015

User-Centered Agile Methods
Hugh Beyer
2010

Experience-Centered Design: Designers, Users, and Communities in Dialogue
Peter Wright and John McCarthy
2010

Experience Design: Technology for All the Right Reasons
Marc Hassenzahl
2010

Designing and Evaluating Usable Technology in Industrial Research: Three Case Studies
Clare-Marie Karat and John Karat
2010

Interacting with Information
Ann Blandford and Simon Attfield
2010

Designing for User Engagement: Aesthetic and Attractive User Interfaces
Alistair Sutcliffe
2009

Context-Aware Mobile Computing: Affordances of Space, Social Awareness, and Social Influence
Geri Gay
2009

Studies of Work and the Workplace in HCI: Concepts and Techniques
Graham Button and Wes Sharrock
2009

Semiotic Engineering Methods for Scientific Research in HCI
Clarisse Sieckenius de Souza and Carla Faria Leitão
2009

Common Ground in Electronically Mediated Conversation
Andrew Monk
2008

Designing for Gesture and Tangible
Interaction Mary Lou Maher and Lina Lee

ISBN: 978-3-031-01091-0 print
ISBN: 978-3-031-02219-7 ebook

DOI 10.1007/978-3-031-02219-7

A Publication in the Springer series
SYNTHESIS LECTURES ON HUMAN-CENTERED INFORMATICS, #36
Series Editors: John M. Carroll, Penn State University

Series ISSN: 1946-7680 Print   1946-7699 Electronic

Designing for Gesture and Tangible Interaction

Mary Lou Maher and Lina Lee
The University of North Carolina at Charlotte

SYNTHESIS LECTURES ON HUMAN-CENTERED INFORMATICS #36

ABSTRACT

Interactive technology is increasingly integrated with physical objects that do not have a traditional keyboard and mouse style of interaction, and many do not even have a display. These objects require new approaches to interaction design, referred to as post-WIMP (Windows, Icons, Menus, and Pointer) or as embodied interaction design.

This book provides an overview of the design opportunities and issues associated with two embodied interaction modalities that allow us to leave the traditional keyboard behind: tangible and gesture interaction. We explore the issues in designing for this new age of interaction by highlighting the significance and contexts for these modalities. We explore the design of tangible interaction with a reconceptualization of the traditional keyboard as a Tangible Keyboard, and the design of interactive three-dimensional (3D) models as Tangible Models. We explore the design of gesture interaction through the design of gesture-base commands for a walk-up-and-use information display, and through the design of a gesture-based dialogue for *the willful marionette*. We conclude with design principles for tangible and gesture interaction and a call for research on the cognitive effects of these modalities.

KEYWORDS

embodied interaction, gesture interaction, tangible interaction, interaction design, cognitive effects

Contents

Preface

This book reflects on the significance and design of embodied interaction with digital information and artifacts. We are experiencing a transition from traditional modes of interacting with computing devices in which we are typically sitting still and moving our fingers on a keyboard to large body movements to effect changes and engage with digital information and artifacts. As designers we are challenged not only by the increasing range of technologies that enable interaction design, but also by the range and focus on human-centered design methodologies. Engineering design starts with requirements derived from human needs but necessarily has a focus on the design of the system so that it satisfies those requirements and optimizes performance of the system. In contrast, in interaction design, the human is inherent to the system and therefor the focus remains on human needs, desires, and abilities throughout the design process. Along with this focus on people during the design of interactive systems, there is an opportunity to move beyond human factors and physical considerations to consider the social and cognitive effects of alternative designs. These opportunities create a new era in interaction design that includes such things as designing gestures and a stronger focus on physical and digital affordances and metaphors. This book is a starting point for understanding the significance of this transition and is a harbinger for future interaction designs in which large body movements are the basis for interaction. Not only is embodied interaction creating new modalities for interaction, it is also redefining the focus of good interaction design by moving away from efficiency and productivity as the basis for interaction design toward the inclusion of creativity and social interaction in the goals for new designs.

Mary Lou Maher and Lina Lee
January 2017

Acknowledgments

This book is a reflection on our collaboration with many colleagues whose views and ideas are tightly woven within our understanding of tangible and gesture interaction. After many years of collaboration, it is hard to untangle our thoughts from the engaging discussions about tangible and gesture interaction. We acknowledge our colleagues here as an integral part of our ability to produce this book. Our understanding of tangible interaction design and our design examples, Tangible Keyboard and Tangible Models, were influenced by Tim Clausner, Mijeong Kim, Alberto Gonzalez, and Kaz Grace. Our understanding of gesture interaction design and our design examples, walk-up-and-use information display and *the willful marionette*, were influenced by collaboration with our artists in residence, Lilla LoCurto and Bill Outcault, and our colleagues Kaz Grace and Mohammad Mahzoon. Lilla and Bill are the artists that imagined, created, and built *the willful marionette*.

Completing this book was possible only with the patience of our families. Our special thanks go to the babies born during this writing project and the many sleepless nights we experienced. We particularly acknowledge the birth of Jessica, Kei, Iris, Matthew, and Erin during the time we were writing this book.

The tangible interaction research reported in this book was partially supported by NSF Grant IIS-1218160: HCC: Small: Designing Tangible Computing for Creativity. The artist-in-residence program that enabled our contribution to *the willful marionette* was supported by the College of Computing and Informatics and the College of Arts and Architecture at UNC Charlotte. We acknowledge the support of the College of Computing and Informatics at UNC Charlotte for funding graduate students and equipment in the InDe Lab.

Mary Lou Maher and Lina Lee
January 2017

CHAPTER 1

Introduction

In this book we explore the design issues for embodied interaction design, and specifically for tangible and gesture interaction. This book describes engaging ways of interacting with tangible and gesture-based interactive systems through four different examples as vehicles for exploring the design issues and methods relevant to embodied interaction design. In recent years, new interaction styles have emerged. Researchers in human-computer interaction (HCI) have explored an embodied interaction that seeks to explain bodily action, human experiences, and physicality in the context of interaction with computational technology (Antle et al., 2009, 2011; Klemmer et al., 2006). Dourish (2004) set out a theoretical foundation of embodiment. The concept of embodiment in tangible user interfaces (TUIs) describes how physical objects may be used simultaneously as input and output for computational processes. Similarly, in gesture-based interaction the concept of embodiment recognizes and takes advantage of the fact that humans have bodies, and people can use those bodies when interacting with technology in the same ways they use them in the natural physical world (Antle et al., 2011). This is an attractive approach to interaction design because it relates to our previous experience and makes it easier to learn new systems.

The success of interaction design depends on providing appropriate methods for the task at hand that improve discoverability and learnability. Designers should consider the user's mental model based on previous experience when defining how the user can interact with the system, and then give the user clues about expected behavior before they take action. Giving feedback to the users is important to make it clear how the user completes an interaction. Since interaction is a conversation between the user(s) and the system, interaction design for gesture input methods and real-time feedback to the user(s) should be very carefully considered. Well-timed, appropriate feedback helps users to notice and understand that the system is interactive, to learn how to interact with it, and to be motivated to interact with it. Ideally, feedback communicates to the user that the system status has altered as the user intended (Dillon, 2003).

As we move toward embodied interaction, we maintain these basic principles of good interaction design: the user initiates interaction with some form of action, and the system responds or alters as the user intended. However, the trend for embodied interaction is the design of very broad and varied ways in which the user is expected to act to initiate interaction, and the iterative action-response needs to be discovered and learned. For example, laptop and touchscreen interactions are ubiquitous enough that there are established guidelines and design patterns that designers adhere to (Norman, 1983). These patterns and guidelines cause users to have certain expectations of how a system might work even before they begin interacting with it. However, embodied interaction is relatively new and does not have as coherent a set of consistent design patterns for interaction. Therefore, we transition from an expectation for consistent and effective interaction design using keyboard, mouse, and display, toward novel interactive systems in which the user explores and learns which actions lead to expected changes in the state of the system. We propose that HCI is a cognitive process in which the user mental model is the basis for their exploration and use of the interactive system. Users decide how to interact on the basis of expectation and prior experience, and the affordances of the specific interactive system modify the user mental model.

As Dourish (2001) says, when users approach an embodied interactive system, they must construct a new understanding of how it works on the basis of their physical exploration. Different people may have unique experiences and expectations, which will affect the way in which they initially explore a system and, ultimately, the mental model they construct of how the system works (Dillon, 2003). Embodied interaction has been used to describe the interactions of users with a wide range of interactive technologies, including tangible and gesture-based interfaces.

We posit that good tangible and gesture interaction design depends on an understanding of the cognitive issues associated with these modalities. We organize these issues into four categories: embodiment, affordances, metaphor, and epistemic actions. These four categories can be used as clues that the designer can give the user to aid the user in understanding how the interactive system is to be operated. If these concepts are integrated into the design process, the user's mental model and knowledge can be activated and extended as they try to use and understand the interactive system. While these cognitive issues require further exploration and empirical validation (Antle et al., 2011), we present specific projects that explore various aspects of embodied HCI.

1.1   EMBODIMENT

Interaction through tangible and gesture-based systems is intrinsically embodied, and therefore decisions about which embodied actions can be recognized by the interactive system are part of the design process. Human gestures are expressive body motions involving physical movements of the fingers, hands, arms, head, face, or body that may convey meaningful information or be performed to interact with the environment (Dan and Mohod, 2014). Designing embodied interaction is not just about designing computing ability, but is also about designing the human experience and anticipated human behavior.

Research has shown that gestures play an integral role in human cognition. Psychologists and cognitive scientists have explored the role of gesture and thought for several decades. McNeil (1992, 2008) explains that gesture and thought are tightly connected, and he also establishes a categorization of gestures and their role in human cognition and communication. There is evidence that gesturing aids thinking. Several studies have shown that learning to count is facilitated by touching physical objects (Efron 1941; Kessell and Tversky 2006; Cook et al., 2008). Kessell and Tversky (2006) show that when people are solving and explaining spatial insight problems, gesturing facilitates finding solutions. Goldin-Meadow and Beilock (2010) summarize findings as "gesture influences thought by linking it to action, (p. 669)" and "producing gesture changes thought (p. 670)" and can "create new knowledge (p. 671)." These studies show that gesture, while originally associated with communication, is also related to thinking. Embodied interaction design creates an environment that is activated by gesture and actions on objects and therefore induces cognitive effects that traditional user interaction does not.

One challenge to embodied interaction is that while it is built upon natural actions, it still requires some level of discovery, especially when it is a public display. Tangible and gesture-based interaction designers consider both the integration of technology and its effects on human experience. The major consideration that has emerged to influence tangible design is the physical embodiment of computing. Interaction design is not just screen-based digital interaction anymore. Tangible interaction designers should think about physical, graspable objects that give cues for understanding and provide the basis for interaction. Gesture interaction designers should think about how various human movements can be recognized and interpreted in the context of changing the state and response of the computational system. Interactive platforms can be interpreted as spaces to act and move in, and they effectively determine interaction patterns.

Dourish (2004) explores the physicality of embodied interaction and its affect on moving human computer interaction toward more social environments. He describes an approach to embodiment grounded in phenomenology, and claims that any understanding we have of the world is the result of some initial physical exploration. Embodied interaction is about establishing meaning and it is through embodied interaction that we develop an understanding of the meaning of the system. As the user constructs their mental model, they are influenced by the phenomena they are experiencing at that moment as well as their prior experiences and understanding of how technology works.

In this book, we take a cognitive view of embodied interaction design: Discovering the interaction model relies on pre-existing mental models derived from physical experiences, and executing intentional physical movements during interaction has an effect on cognition. We demonstrate and elaborate on this view of embodiment through four projects; where we describe the gestures that enable interaction, the design methods, and the usability issues for each project.

1.2   AFFORDANCE

The concept of affordance was introduced to the HCI community by Norman (1988) and Gibson (1982). According to Norman (1988), an affordance is the design aspect of an object that allows people to know how to use it and that gives a clue to its function and use. Norman discusses the concept of affordance as properties of an object that allow specific actions such as a handle affords holding and turning, a button affords pressing and make it its own function clear. Tangible interaction design is arguably more influenced by physical affordances than by visual or gesture interaction design.

TUIs change the way we interact with digital information, with physical affordances that are distinctly different from pointing and keyboard/mouse interaction. According to Wang et al. (2002), there are two advantages to tangible interaction; first, it allows direct, naïve manipulability and intuitive understanding; and second, the sense of touch provides an additional dimension. The tactile feedback afforded by TUIs is consistent with the early empiricist argument that kinesthetic information provides us with the ability to construct a spatial map of objects that we touch (Lederman and Klatzky, 1993; Loomis and Lederman, 1986). Fitzmaurice (Fitzmaurice, 1996; Fitzmaurice and Buxton, 1997) demonstrated that having multiple graspable interactive devices encourages two-handed interaction that calls upon everyday coordination skills. Leganchuk et al. (1998) explored the potential benefits of such two-handed input through experimental tasks to find that bimanual manipulation may bring two types of advantages to HCI: manual and cognitive. The two-handed interaction doubles the freedom simultaneously available to the user and reduces the cognitive load of the input performance.

The potential affordances of the TUIs, such as manipulability and physical arrangements, may reduce cognitive load associated with spatial reasoning, thus resulting in enhanced spatial cognition and creative cognition. Brereton and McGarry (2000) studied the role of objects in supporting design thinking as a precursor to designing tangible interaction; they found that design thinking is dependent on gesturing with objects, and recommend that the design of tangible devices consider a tradeoff between exploiting the ambiguous and varied affordances of specific physical objects. The affordances of design tools facilitate specific aspects of designing. As we move away from the traditional WIMP (Windows, Icons, Menus, and Pointer) interaction, we encounter new kinds of affordances in interactive digital design tools (Burlamaqui and Dong, 2015). Tangible interaction design takes advantage of natural physical affordances (Ishii and Ullmer, 1997) by exploiting the knowledge that people already have from their experience with nondigital objects to design novel forms of interacting and discovering. In this book, we focus on the affordances of the interaction that can be sensed by the interactive devices. Well-designed objects make it clear how they work just by looking at them. The successful design of embodied interaction systems does not ignore the affordances of the physical and visual aspects of the system.

1.3   METAPHOR

While affordances of physical objects are closely related to our experience with their physical properties, the properties of tangible interaction objects have both physical and digital relationships. In contrast to physical objects, on-screen objects are clusters of pixels without a physical dimension.

A common way to create the appearance of physical affordances to on screen objects is the use of metaphor in designing interface elements (Szabó, 1995). By creating a visual reference on screen to familiar physical objects, the on-screen objects take on some of the affordances of the metaphorical object (Mohnkern, 1997).

The use of a metaphor during design makes familiar that which is unknown or unfamiliar by connecting it with the user's previous experience (Dillon, 2003). The most well-known is the "desktop metaphor" used in current operating systems. Another common example of metaphor is the trash can. You can grab a file with the mouse to take it above the trash can and release it. A designer can use the shape, the size, the color, the weight, and the texture of the object to invoke any number of metaphorical links (Fishkin, 2004).

Metaphors are an important concept for embodied interaction. An interaction model based on embodied metaphors effectively implements a mapping between action and output that is consistent with the metaphorical object. Through design, we can map human behaviors and bodily experiences onto abstract concepts in interactive environments (Bakker et al., 2012). Metaphor gives users a known model for an unknown system. Metaphor can help ease the transition to a new situation, so it is good for creating systems that will be used primarily by novices, like public displays. For embodied interaction design, in which there are few standards and fewer user manuals, the role of metaphor in design may be critical in creating easily discovered and learnable interactive systems.

1.4   EPISTEMIC ACTIONS

Epistemic action is exploratory motor activity aimed at uncovering information that is hard to compute mentally. Kirsh and Maglio (1994) distinguish between epistemic and pragmatic actions. A pragmatic action is the action needed to actually perform the task. Epistemic actions are actions that help the person explore the task and guide them to the solution. As such, epistemic actions enable the person to use physical objects and their environment to aid their cognition (Kirsh and Maglio, 1994; van den Hoven and Mazalek, 2011). Therefore, having a variety of tangible objects and physical arrangements may aid problem solving while interacting with a tangible interactive system. Fitzmaurice (1996) discussed the concepts of pragmatic and epistemic actions to provide the underlying theoretical support for workable graspable user interfaces (UIs). Pragmatic action refers to performatory motor activity that directs the user toward to the final goal. Epistemic action refers to exploratory motor activity that may uncover hidden information that would otherwise require a great deal of mental computation.

Kim and Maher (2007) found an increase of epistemic actions in a design task while using a tangible UI, and through a protocol analysis, were able to also observe an increase in the cognitive processes typically associated with creative design. The projects in this book build on that result to design tangible interfaces based on physical objects that offer more opportunities for epistemic (i.e., exploratory) actions than pragmatic (i.e., performatory) actions. Exploration through epistemic actions enables a better perception of the environment and supports learning more about the properties of the objects. When designing gesture-based interaction, the process of discovering the interaction model can be leveraged by encouraging and responding to epistemic actions.

1.5   THIS BOOK

In this book we present tangible and gesture interaction design with an underlying assumption that embodiment, affordances, metaphor, and epistemic actions are critical cognitive issues that can influence the quality of the design. If the interaction design is not well conceived with respect to these cognitive issues, users suffer from frustration, discomfort, stress, and fatigue. Applying appropriate design methods is crucial and should help bridge the differences between the designer's view of the system and user's mental model. It is important to conduct user research to know how to incorporate the insights from users' experiences into the design. In this book, various user research and design methods such as gesture elicitation, protocol analysis, heuristic evaluation, prototyping, body-storming, role-playing, personas, and image boards are described to show how designers understand the potential user mental models of the interactive system. We describe these methods in the context of their use in the four design examples: Tangible Keyboard, Tangible Models, walk-up-and-use information display, and *the willful marionette*.

This book can provide HCI practitioners and researchers with new principles for better designs and new ideas for research in embodied interaction. For HCI practitioners, the book describes specific design projects and the methods used during design and evaluation. These methods are specific to designing for tangible and gesture interaction. The description of these methods will help practitioners understand how these methods are applied, and, when appropriate, how these methods are uniquely suited to tangible and gesture interaction. For the HCI researcher, the book identifies the cognitive and design research issues that are raised when designing for tangible and gesture interaction. Many of the methods described in the design projects are also applicable in a research context.

The organization of this book is as follows: Chapter 2 presents the concepts and significance of tangible interaction design. In Chapter 3, we present a description of our experience in designing the Tangible Keyboard and Tangible Models. Gesture interaction design is presented in terms of the technology and significance in Chapter 4. We follow this with a description of our experience in designing the walk-up-and-use information display and *the willful marionette* in Chapter 5. In Chapter 6, we conclude with our understanding of the research challenges in designing for embodied interaction design.

CHAPTER 2

Tangible Interaction Design

2.1 WHAT IS A TANGIBLE INTERACTION?

Tangible User Interfaces (TUIs) have emerged as an interface and interaction style that links the digital and physical worlds (Ullmer and Ishii, 2000; Shaer and Hornecker, 2010). An early definition of tangible interaction was introduced by Ishii and Ullmer (1997) as an extension of the idea of graspable user interfaces (UIs): they argued that tangible interaction allows users to grasp and manipulate bits by coupling digital information with physical objects and architectural surfaces.

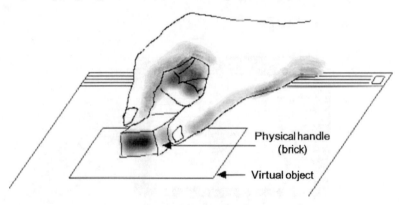

Figure 2.1: Graspable object. Based on Fitzmaurice (1996, p. 4).

TUIs employ physical objects with a direct correlation to digital objects as an alternative to traditional computer input and output devices for control (e.g., mouse) and display (e.g., screen) (Fishkin, 2004). A person uses their hands to manipulate one or more physical objects via gestures and actions such as pointing, clicking, holding, and grasping. A computer system detects the movement, changes its state, and provides feedback (Petridis et al., 2006). TUIs are designed to build on our experience and skills from interacting with the non-digital world (Ishii and Ullmer, 1997; Shaer and Jacob, 2009). TUIs offer the possibility of natural interfaces that are intuitive and enjoyable to use as well as easy to learn (Shaer, 2008). TUIs have the potential to enhance learning and problem solving by changing the way people interact with and leverage digital information (Shaer and Jacob, 2009). Current research in tangible interaction includes understanding the design and cognitive implications of TUIs, developing new technologies that further bridge the digital and the physical, and guiding TUI design with knowledge gained from empirical studies.

The goal of this chapter is to provide an overview and general framework for the design of tangible interaction, including consideration of the role of gesture and the impact on cognition. We believe that TUIs have an impact on cognition because they provide affordances that encourage and facilitate specific gestures and actions, making some cognitive activities easier. TUIs change the way we interact with digital information via physical affordances that are distinctly different from pointing and keyboard/mouse interaction. This chapter explores physical manipulation as an interaction design space. TUIs trigger various gestures and have potential for exploring information through novel forms of interacting and discovering. The chapter presents the concepts and design issues of TUIs through two examples: the Tangible Keyboard and Tangible Models. They exemplify two approaches to integrating TUIs with traditional interaction design: the Tangible Keyboard design examines the metaphor of a keyboard where each key is a tangible object; Tangible Models design examines physical interaction with 3D objects as proxies for 3D digital models.

2.1.1   TANGIBLE KEYBOARD

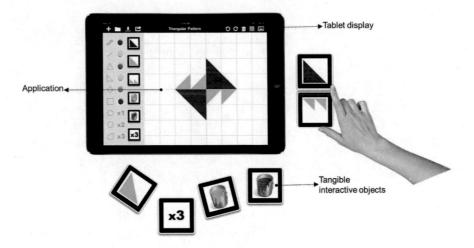

Figure 2.2: Pattern Maker application on the Tangible Keyboard. Tangible Keyboard video available on: https://drive.google.com/file/d/0B4S5ptYjjjuGbFEyX2ljUk90LVU/view?usp=sharing.

Tangible Keyboard is a tangible computing platform that adopts a keyboard metaphor in developing tangible devices for touch screen tablets. The tangible interaction design has a focus on supporting composition tasks and the potential for enhancing creative cognition through spatial arrangement. The Tangible Keyboard design provides separate interaction spaces for composition tasks: the whole composition is displayed on the tablet, and the individual pieces of the composition are manipulated on tangible interactive objects. Individual elements are displayed on tangible interactive objects (inspired by Sifteo cubes™), and these smaller displays are manipulated to create a composition on a larger touch display tablet (Merrill et al., 2012). A variety of different gestures and actions on the tangible objects serve as the basis for the interaction design of the Tangible Keyboard. The larger display on a tablet provides visual feedback for compositions and the touch screen allows users to interact with on-screen content. The affordances of the Tangible Keyboard build on the idea of creating keys, similar to the keys on a keyboard, where the symbols on the keys are interactive, and the keys can be rearranged to create variety of creative patterns. Figure 2.2 illustrates the Tangible Keyboard design with the Pattern Maker application.

2.1.2   TANGIBLE MODELS

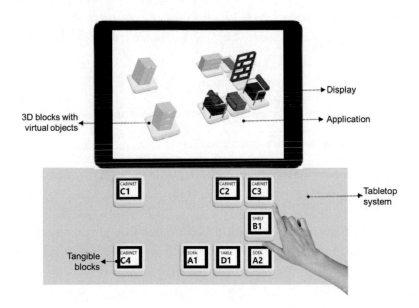

Figure 2.3: Tangible Models interaction design for CAD modeling.

Tangible Models is a tangible computing platform that combines a touchscreen tabletop system with augmented reality that integrates tangible objects on a horizontal display to support 3D configuration design tasks (Kim and Maher, 2008). This tabletop system provides a physical and digital environment for co-located design collaboration. The tabletop system runs a computer-aided design (CAD) program to display a plan view of a 3D design, with physical augmented reality blocks representing objects and their placement on the plan view. Tangible Models interaction design uses 3D blocks with markers that reference 3D models in the ARToolKit (https://artoolkit.org/). Using ArchiCAD (http://www.graphisoft.com/archicad/), Tangible Models allows the user to arrange 3D models from a library, such as walls, doors, and furniture. The ArchiCAD library provides pre-designed 3D objects that can be selected, adapted, and placed in the new design. Tangible Models interaction design comprises selection and rearrangement actions on blocks to explore alternative configuration designs. By rearranging 3D models as physical actions on blocks, the affordances of this UI reduces cognitive load by providing direct manipulability and intuitive understanding of the spatial relationships of the components of the design. Figure 2.3 illustrates the Tangible Models platform using 3D models of furniture from the ArchiCAD library.

2.2 WHY IS TANGIBLE INTERACTION INTERESTING?

TUIs represent a departure from conventional computing by connecting digital information with graspable objects in the physical world (Fishkin, 2004). Fitzmaurice (1996) defines five core properties as the major differences between tangible interaction devices and mouse/keyboard interaction devices:

1. space-multiplexing of both input and output;

2. concurrent access and manipulation of interface components;

3. strong specific devices;

4. spatially-aware computational devices; and

5. spatial re-configurability of devices.

A hallmark of TUIs is specialized physical/digital devices that provide concurrent access to multiple input devices that can control interface widgets as well as afford physical manipulation and spatial arrangement of digital information and models (Fitzmaurice, 1996; Fitzmaurice and Buxton, 1997; Shaer and Hornecker, 2010). These characteristics affect the way tangible interaction is designed. In addition, tangible interaction is contextual: the design is strongly affected by the context of use. The Tangible Keyboard is designed for composition of elements that do not have a corresponding 3D physical object, such as words, numbers, or 2D shapes. The Tangible Models platform is designed for the composition of elements that have a 3D physical counterpart. We explore these 5 factors and their characteristics to better understand design principles for TUI in the context of the Tangible Keyboard and Tangible Models.

2.2.1 SPACE-MULTIPLEXED INPUT AND OUTPUT

Space-multiplexed input and output involves having multiple physical objects, each specific to a function and independently accessible (Ullmer and Ishii, 1997). Time-multiplexed input and output occurs when only one input device is available (for example, the mouse): the user has to repeatedly select and deselect objects and functions (Shaer and Hornecker, 2010). For example, the mouse is used to control different interaction functions such as menu selection, scrolling windows, pointing, and clicking buttons in a time-sequential manner (Jacko, 2012). TUIs are space-multiplexed because they typically provide multiple input devices that are spatially aware or whose location can be sensed by the system. As a result, input and output devices are distributed over space, enabling the user to select a digital object or function by grasping a physical object (Shaer and Hornecker, 2010; Patten and Ishii, 2007).

1) Tangible Keyboard

Tangible Keyboard has space-multiplexed input/output devices, which enables graspable rearrangement of the elements of a composition. This design provides a distinct approach to composition that is not supported by the traditional keyboard or mouse owing to the ability to manually rearrange subsets of a composition and control the content on the subset being manipulated by referring to the composition on a larger display. With space-multiplexed input, each function to be controlled has a dedicated transducer, each occupying its own space (Fitzmaurice and Buxton, 1997). For example, in a Pattern Maker application on the Tangible Keyboard, each cube can be used to manipulate a shape, a color, and a scaling function. While the input devices are used to manipulate and input the composition, they also provide a visualization of subsets of the composition that can be repeated or rearranged as input.

2) Tangible Models

Tangible Models also has space-multiplexed input/output devices. The individual input/output blocks are each associated with a 3D digital model that is visible on the vertical display. The 3D models are rearranged on the tabletop in reference to a plan view of the composition, with visual feedback of the 3D scene on the vertical display. These multiple 3D blocks allow direct control of digital objects as space-multiplexed input devices, each specific to a function and independently accessible. The application of Tangible Models to the configuration design of rooms on a floor plan layout allows the user to assign 3D models such as walls and furniture from a library to each block. The user can rearrange the blocks to explore various design configurations by reaching for and moving the block as a handle for the 3D model.

2.2.2   CONCURRENCY

A core property of TUIs is space-multiplexed input and output. This allows for simultaneous, but independent and potentially persistent selection of objects. TUIs have multiple devices available, and interactions that allow for concurrent access and manipulation of interface components (Fitzmaurice, 1996). In a traditional graphical user interface (GUI), one active selection is possible at a time and a new selection should be done in order to undo a prior one. Time-multiplexed input devices have no physical contextual awareness and lack the efficiency of specialized tools. The ability to use a single device for several tasks is a major benefit of the GUI, but given the nature of interaction, where only one person can edit the model at a time, the GUI environment may change interactivity in collaborative design (Magerkurth and Peter, 2002). However, TUIs can possibly eliminate many of the redundant selection actions and make selections easier. In terms of collaborative interactions, the TUI environment enables designers to collaborate on handling the physical objects more interactively by allowing concurrent access with multiple points of control (Maher and Kim, 2005).

1) Tangible Keyboard

Tangible Keyboard focuses on the user experience during a creative task in which the user has multiple tangible objects that are manipulated to compose and synthesize elements of new design. Multiple tangible objects offer greater flexibility, allowing each input device to display different types of function. In the Pattern Maker application, each input device displays a single shape, color, or scale. A shape can also be modified on a cube by rearranging these different shapes, colors, and scales. Shape cubes can be manipulated independently but also modified with color or scale cubes to create new design patterns. Concurrency is achieved through simultaneous access to multiple physical devices where each one displays its own shape, color, or scale.

2) Tangible Models

Tangible Models provides a similar experience, but with each tangible object assuming the geometric properties of a 3D object. The spatial rearrangement of the 3D models is directly correlated with the 3D composition. Concurrency is achieved through simultaneous access to multiple 3D models, each on a separate physical object. A protocol study of designers using Tangible Models, described in Kim and Maher (2008), showed that users were more focused on the spatial and functional relationships among the individual 3D objects than on the properties of each object when compared to an interaction design that was time-multiplexed (keyboard and mouse). With the direct, naïve manipulability of physical objects and rapid visualization, designers in the TUI environment produced more cognitive actions and completed the design tasks faster.

2.2.3 STRONG SPECIFIC DEVICES

TUIs provide strong specific devices for interacting with the system. This offers more efficiency because the tangible objects are designed to be more specialized and tailored for working on a given task in order to increase the directness and intuitiveness of interactions (Le Goc et al., 2015;

Hornecker, 2005). The design of appropriate physical representations is a very important aspect of tangible interface design (Ullmer and Ishii, 2000). To create strong specific devices, the most common approach is to utilize existing objects into which position sensors or ID tags are inserted. Alternatively, strong specific devices are achieved with Augmented Reality (AR), where each physical device is associated with a virtual object. The user interacts with a virtual object by manipulating the corresponding physical object (Waldner et al., 2006). While seeing virtual imagery superimposed on physical objects, the user perceives interaction with the digital object. These specialized interactive objects may lack generality and therefore may not be effective for some tasks. This loss of generality may be overcome by the advantages provided by task-specific physical tools (Fitzmaurice, 1996). Tangible user interaction with physical objects that have a specialized form and appearance offer affordances normally associated only with the physical object.

1) Tangible Keyboard

In the case of the Tangible Keyboard, the form is constant (cube-like objects with a display) and the appearance (display) is variable. The image on the display is designed to fit the context of the tasks supported by the application. The affordances of these specific devices are those associated with the shape of the object and the content on the display. In the Pattern Maker application, shape cubes are rearranged to form patterns and color cubes are tilted to pour a new color on a shape. These strong specific devices do not have the generality of the mouse for selecting any function, but provide strong feedback on the functions enabled by the application.

2) Tangible Models

With Tangible Models, simple 3D blocks as tangible devices are rearranged on a tabletop system with a vertical display of the 3D scene. Each block is associated with a single 3D model, providing a strong specific device for creating a composition of a scene or spatial design. With static mappings and multiple input objects, 3D blocks as tangible input elements can be expressive and provide affordances specific to the object they represent. The visualization of each 3D block directly indicates its meaning or function while the user is moving the pieces and making a composition.

2.2.4   SPATIALLY AWARE COMPUTATIONAL DEVICES

Spatially aware computational devices and spatial configurations are important concepts in embodied interaction. A physical object in TUIs is typically aware of its spatial position and is registered with a central processing unit. Both position and orientation are critical pieces of information to be sensed (Fitzmaurice, 1996; Valdes et al., 2014). Proximity information is possible through communication to a central processing unit or independent sensors on each device. Applications that are more graphic than alphanumeric benefit from having spatially aware input devices, as graphical tasks are inherently spatial in nature (Fitzmaurice, 1996). Spatially aware computational devices allow users to interact with complex information spaces in a physical way by changing the spatial position and orientation of tangible devices.

1) Tangible Keyboard

Tangible Keyboard is built on the hardware/software platform of Sifteo cubes™ and the sensors include adjacency awareness and accelerometers. These sensors allow the cubes to be aware of other cubes and the movements of each cube, such as shaking, tilting, and turning over. By communicating with a central processor, the rearrangement and movements of the cubes can be mapped onto input events related to the composition task. For the Pattern Maker application, spatial awareness of the individual devices allows the user to form compositions and to modify the shape, color, and scale of elements of the composition.

2) Tangible Models

Tangible Models is built on the software platform of the ARToolkit, in which spatial awareness is achieved by a camera that senses the location of predefined markers (Kato et al., 2001). The assignment of each marker to a 3D model allows the superposition of the visualization of the 3D model on the block. The identification of a marker in the physical space sensed by the camera allows the movement of the block in the physical space to be tracked and visualized in the digital space and displayed on the tabletop for the plan view and on the vertical screen for the perspective view.

2.2.5   SPATIAL RECONFIGURABILITY OF DEVICES

Tangible objects are discrete, spatially reconfigurable physical objects that represent and control digital information. Tangible objects enable reconfiguration, which provides the feeling that users are actually holding and rearranging the information itself. According to Fitzmaurice (1996), the spatial reconfiguration of physical elements such as placement, removal, orientation, and translation are the modes of interaction with tangible interfaces. Those physical controls generally communicate with the surrounding environment and contribute to its overall function and use. The value of discrete, spatially reconfigurable interactive devices goes beyond the value in grasping and rearranging the devices because the physicality of the device serves as a cognitive aid by providing an external cue for a particular function or data item. Users can rapidly reconfigure and rearrange the devices in a workspace and customize their space to suit their own needs in task workflows and task switching (Fitzmaurice, 1996). While this can be achieved in some WIMP interfaces, the use of tangible devices makes this reconfiguration as simple as holding the device and moving it to a new location.

1) Tangible Keyboard

Tangible Keyboard enables configuration of elements within an application or across applications. In the Pattern Maker application, each cube can represent a shape, color, or scale. Within that application, the display and meaning of a specific cube can be changed from a shape to a color to a scale. Across applications, when, for example, comparing the Pattern Maker application to the Silly Poems application, the display on a cube can be changed from a shape to a word. Seeing the Tangible Keyboard, even when it is not being used, conveys an interaction design of physical manipulation and spatial configuration of the physical elements within the interaction design.

2) Tangible Models

Tangible Models enables configuration of models within or across applications. Within an application, the 3D model associated with each block can be changed by selecting another object from the library to assign to a specific block. Across applications, the 3D models available to be selected for each block can be changed by selecting a different library of models. If configuring a structural engineering design, the library would comprise beams, columns, and floor panels instead of furniture and walls. Seeing a Tangible Models device, even when it is not being used, conveys an interaction design of physical manipulation due to the physical presence of blocks on a tabletop system.

2.3   WHAT ARE KEY DESIGN ISSUES FOR TANGIBLE USER INTERFACES?

TUIs show promise to significantly enhance computer-mediated support for a variety of application domains, including learning, problem solving, and entertainment. Also, TUIs offer the possibility of interfaces that are easy to learn and use. However, TUIs are currently considered challenging to design and build owing to a lack of existing software applications that can take advantage of continuous and parallel interactions, the lack of standard interaction models and abstractions for TUIs, and the need to cross disciplinary boundaries to effectively link the physical and digital worlds (Shaer et al., 2004; Shaer and Hornecker, 2010). This section discusses four design issues of TUIs based on Shaer and Jacob (2009);

1. designing interplay of virtual and physical;

2. selecting from multiple gestures and actions;

3. crossing disciplinary boundaries; and

4. the lack of standard input and output interaction models.

Explorations of these design issues provide us with an increasingly clearer picture of the strengths and limitations of TUIs. Good design aims to bring out the strengths and to alleviate weaknesses. In this section, we discuss some of the design issues of TUIs. However, it is important to note that TUI research is a growing and rapidly evolving field, and our understanding of the implications of TUI design requires further investigation. Building a TUI is a complex process that encompasses multidisciplinary knowledge, including computer science, design, and cognitive sciences. Many researchers and interaction designers have introduced a variety of techniques for designing and building novel TUIs. However, TUIs are not yet widely used commercially. Yet TUIs provide physical interfaces that have greater potential to reduce cognitive load and offer an intuitive interaction to support activities such as learning, problem solving, and design.

2.3.1   DESIGNING INTERPLAY OF VIRTUAL AND PHYSICAL

TUIs can be considered a specific implementation of the original notion of ubiquitous computing, which aimed at allowing users to remain situated in the real world, while retaining the primacy of the physical world (Shaer and Hornecker, 2010; Wellner et al., 1993; Leigh et al., 2015). Since TUIs provide physical objects in order to interact with the virtual environment, they rely on metaphors that give physical form to digital information. The TUI designer determines which information is best represented digitally and which is best represented physically (Shaer and Jacob, 2009; Bakker et al., 2012; Want et al., 1999). Tangible Models is good example, because this platform uses augmented reality where digital images are superimposed on tangible blocks blending reality with virtuality. The ARToolKit is used to rapidly develop augmented reality applications. Spatially manipulated tangible blocks sit and operate on a large horizontal display. When designers manipulate multiple blocks, each block allows direct control of a virtual object by communicating digital information visually to the user. Through manipulating 3D tangible blocks, the designers also gain tactile feedback from their interaction (Abdelmohsen and Do, 2007; Anderson et al., 2000). TUI developers consider design issues such as physical syntax (Ullmer, 2002), dual feed-back loop (digital and physical), perceived coupling (the extent to which the link between user action and systems response is clear) (Hornecker and Buur, 2006), and observability (the extent to which the physical state of the system indicates its internal state) to make physical interaction devices understandable (Shaer and Jacob, 2009). It is a challenge to develop frameworks to provide the vocabulary for developing TUIs that link the virtual and physical. Therefore, the discussion, comparison, and refinement of designs with respect to these issues is often performed in an ad-hoc way that does not facilitate generalization (Shaer and Jacob, 2009).

Figure 2.4: (a) BUILD-IT bricks. Used with permission (Fjeld et al., 1997); (b) Interior Design application paddle. Used with permission (Kato et al., 2001); (c) ARTHUR wand. Used with permission (Nielsen et al., 2003).

1) Tangible Keyboard

The Tangible Keyboard design addresses these considerations in the following ways: The physical syntax is that of a Sifteo Cube expressed as a rectangular disc with a display. The affordances of these devices include grasping, neighboring, tilting, and pressing. The application provides feedback from the physical interaction through changes in the visual display on the cube as well as on the tablet. Audio and haptic feedback also confirms a digital response to a physical action. In this design, based on the Sifteo cubes™ platform, the interplay between the physical and the digital is visual, tactile, haptic, and audible.

2) Tangible Models

The Tangible Models design addresses the interplay of physical and digital through visual feedback only; since the physical location is sensed via a camera, the feedback from the system is entirely visual. The movement of a physical device is seen on the display as the camera displays the movement. The emergence of a 3D model from a physical block device is achieved by sensing the marker on the physical device and superimposing the 3D model on the location of the marker. In this system, based on the ARToolkit, the interplay between the physical and digital is tactile and visual.

2.3.2   SELECTING FROM MULTIPLE GESTURES AND ACTIONS

A TUI designer needs to define an interaction model comprising a user action–system response pair for each possible context of use. In the physical world, there are numerous actions that can be performed with any physical object (Shaer and Jacob, 2009). The interaction model for TUI defines which actions are meaningful in which context. The designer needs to develop this interaction model, effectively communicate it to users, and then implement a solution for computationally sensing these actions. There are no strong conventions or general interaction models to represent a set of gestures for TUIs. Gesture-elicitation studies provide a methodology for designing gestures and actions in the interaction model that match user expectations and suggestions for gesture interaction.

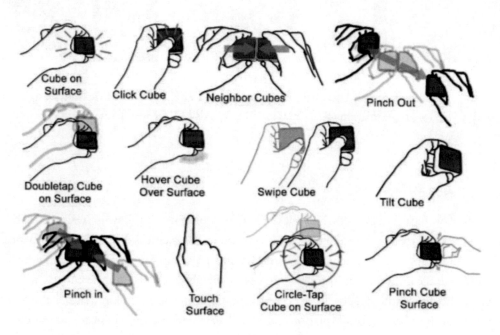

Figure 2.5: User-generated gesture vocabulary. Used with permission from Valdes et al., 2014, p. 4111).

In the broad sense, gestures are meaningful hand movements, and therefore the movement of hands as actions in TUIs can be considered gesture (van den Hoven and Mazalek, 2011). Emerging evidence suggests that together, gesture and language behaviors express a common cognitive/neural processing system for linking meaning with symbols, whether these are words, gestures, images, sounds, or objects (Xu et al., 2009). Multiple behaviors and actions are used to design the interaction in TUI systems.

1) Tangible Keyboard

In designing the Tangible Keyboard, the focus was on defining the meaning for moving two cubes next to each other, pressing on the display of a cube, tilting a cube, and shaking a cube. The interaction design includes pointing to icons and menu items on the tablet. The design of the interactive system was achieved through iterations on the selection of the gestures and actions and their associated interpretation by the software application. This is described in more detail in Chapter 5.

2) Tangible Models

In designing the Tangible Models platform, the focus was on providing visual feedback on the association between each block and a 3D model. The actions on the blocks are interpreted only by how an action changes the physical location of a block within the 3D digital model of the room or building being designed. This is because of the use of a camera to sense the location of the tangible devices in space and the lack of sensors for other physical manipulations. In this system the interaction design decisions were much simpler: the user can move the 3D block anywhere within view of the camera and see the effect of the movement on the display. This approach to implementing tangible interaction is similar to the Osmo application (https://www.playosmo.com/en/), where there are strong specific devices as physical objects whose movements are seen superimposed on the digital display.

2.3.3   CROSSING DISCIPLINARY BOUNDARIES

Designing and building a TUI requires cross-disciplinary knowledge, including computer science, design, and cognitive sciences (Shaer and Jacob, 2009). Tangible interaction design and implementation spans a variety of perspectives, such as HCI engineering and interaction design, but specializes on interfaces or systems that are in some way embodied in physical artifacts or in environments (Zigelbaum and Csikszentmihályi, 2007). Furthermore, tangible interactions have connections with product design, industrial design, arts, and architecture. New developments in ubiquitous computing, actuation, sensors, robotics, and mechanics contribute to tangible interaction with enabling technologies (Fjeld et al., 1997). Thus, TUIs are often developed by interdisciplinary teams. While each discipline contributes skills necessary for building TUIs, the collaboration is challenged by the different terminologies and work practices.

1) Tangible Keyboard

The design of the Tangible Keyboard drew on knowledge from HCI design, cognitive psychology, and software design. We iterated on the selection and mapping of users' actions and system responses informed by our experimental studies of participants interacting with cubes, tablets, and paper while performing configuration tasks (Maher et al., 2014). We used heuristic analysis studies to inform our assumptions and decisions about the affordances of the cubes and their association with specific system responses. We did not design the hardware configuration of the Sifteo cubes™, which would require knowledge about sensors, microprocessors, haptics, and HCI engineering.

2) Tangible Models

The design of the Tangible Models platform drew on knowledge from HCI design, software design, and architectural design. We developed the design following the existing interaction design of CAD systems, and ArchiCAD in particular. In this design, the decisions were limited because we replaced the keyboard and mouse for selection and for the movement of 3D models with blocks that were already associated with a model, and because of the simplicity of moving the model by moving the block on a table. We did not design the sensor technology because we used the AR-Toolkit platform.

2.3.4 THE LACK OF STANDARD INPUT AND OUTPUT INTERACTION MODELS

Touch interaction design has achieved a consistency across applications. In contrast, there is very little consistency in the interaction models for TUIs. The design of interaction models for TUIs has yet to take into account a common set of heuristics to develop consistency across applications. Most user actions are consistent with the physical world, such as using gravity and other affordances. However, we found inconsistent pairings of user and system actions across application platforms. For example, some applications use Press for changing object or screen and others use Flip for the same result. Moreover, some applications use Press to trigger an action and others use Flip for the same action. The interaction model for some applications is a bad match between system and real world for instance, an application that uses "throw" for spinning an object.

1) Tangible Keyboard

Designing the Tangible Keyboard required several iterations owing to the lack of a standard interaction model. Many of our early designs received many negative usability concerns during our usability testing because it is not obvious to the user what each action (neighbor, tilt, press, etc.) means. While the designers could agree on a meaningful association between a gesture or user action and its mapping to a system action or response, different users had different expectations.

2) Tangible Models

Designing the Tangible Models did not rely on a standard interaction model because the actions were limited to moving the blocks in space, and the system provided immediate visual feedback. This tangible interaction design was simplified by the lack of sensors for any other actions and the reliance on a camera for movement and location of the tangible blocks.

CHAPTER 3

Designing for Tangible Interaction

While there are several descriptions of the methods and issues in interaction design (Sharp, 2003; Hanington and Martin, 2012; Schmidt, 2010), there are fewer articles and books devoted to the design issues specifically associated with tangible interaction design. Since designing for tangible interaction is highly context dependent, we review some common design issues in the context of our two design examples: the Tangible Keyboard and Tangible Models. For each example, we highlight the context of use and its impact on the design, the design goals for each example design, the decisions around the selection of a technical solution for enabling specific aspects of tangible interaction, the relevant design methods, and the designing interaction model. For each example, we summarize and conclude with guidelines for future similar designs.

3.1   DESIGNING THE TANGIBLE KEYBOARD

3.1.1   CONTEXT OF USE

The Tangible Keyboard supports composition in a creative design task in which the user can arrange and manipulate elements of a composition using multiple tangible objects. Hands-on manipulation of tangible objects can guide attention to problem structure and engages creative thinking because moving objects during problem solving offloads information onto physical objects, and therefore may be an aid to thinking about spatial relationships. The user of the Tangible Keyboard platform makes a design pattern by arranging tangible cubes. A tablet displays the shapes' composition in progress, while the cubes support exploration with the components of the composition in a larger, three-dimensional space. A shape can also be modified on a cube by applying these different shapes, colors, and scales.

The context of use for the Tangible Keyboard can be illustrated with three different applications: composition of shapes, words, and sounds, as described below. In each of these applications, we refer to an object cube that is an element of the composition and a control cube that is a modifier for each element.

1) Compositions of Shapes

Pattern Maker is a prototype application that demonstrates how the Tangible Keyboard can support composing new patterns. Example tasks include: designing a composite shape from prescribed elemental shapes, composing mazes, creating graph structures, and designing floor plans or buildings. Each of these applications assumes a different range of shape-related elements on the object and control cubes.

Figure 3.1: Pattern Maker application for the compositions of shapes.

2) Compositions of Words

Silly Poems is a prototype application that demonstrates how the Tangible Keyboard platform can support writing limericks. Going beyond limericks, the Tangible Keyboard can support creative writing when the elements are words, for example, composing poetry, writing stories, composing phrases to describe illustrations, and playing word combination games. Each of these applications assumes a different range of word related elements on the object and control cubes.

Figure 3.2: Silly Poems application for the compositions of words.

3) Compositions of Sounds

Making Music is an application for composing music. Here, the "keys" represent individual sounds or notes, or music notation. Users can explore the different arrangements of musical notes, melodies, and chords, and apply controls that change the pitch, timbre, volume, etc. Musical composition applications assume a different range of music-related elements on the object and control cubes.

Figure 3.3: Making Music application for the composition of sounds.

3.1.2   DESIGN GOALS

The primary design goal of the Tangible Keyboard is to create a user experience for creative composition in which the user has multiple tangible objects that are manipulated to compose and synthesize elements of a new design. Tangible Keyboard is a design that builds on the familiarity of the keyboard, but instead of requiring that our hands stay still, encourages the user to move and gesture with their hands to interact with a creative composition being displayed on the tablet display screen. In summary, the design goals are:

- tangible interaction with elements of a creative composition;

- separation of spaces for tangible interaction with elements of the composition and touch interaction with the whole composition;

- encouragement of hand movements, such as gesture and action, on objects; and

- an easy-to-discover interaction model

3.1.3   TECHNOLOGY SELECTION

1) Tangible Interactive Objects

For the "keys," we selected the Sifteo cubes™: these are existing tangible computing devices that have a digital display, sensors, and communication interfaces, illustrated in Figure 3.4. As tangible interactive objects, the cubes have a graspable, multi-gesture interactive interface. Users can physically experiment with different combinations of the pieces of their composition and rearrange their positions in a 2D space. The cubes can wirelessly communicate with each other and with the composition. Using the metaphor of the keyboard, the cubes become "graspable keys," where each cube is an interactive and content-varied key that provides the user's input to the composition. Sifteo™ cubes can be programmed to virtually be any object. As a result, the composition on the screen can be made up of a variety of different objects. Additionally, each cube provides feedback to the user when actions are performed on the cube. Therefore, users can focus on individual components of the composition or on the composition.

Figure 3.4: Sifteo cubes™ Tangible User Interface cubes. From Maher et al. (2016), used with permission.

2) Tablet Display

The display size of the cubes limits the amount of media and content that can be presented or controlled by the user. The small screen size of the cube also restricts the user from seeing the bigger picture, which is necessary when creating compositions. The application programming interface (API) for the cubes provides the software interface to the physical device and allows Tangible Keyboard to code the interpretation of various actions on the cubes. The larger display on a tablet provides visual feedback for compositions, and the touch screen allows users to interact with on-screen content. The API for the tablet display provides a software interface for the interaction with the composition through touch interaction.

3.1.4 DESIGN METHODS

We initiated our design process as a metaphorical design with reference to the keyboard. This provided a conceptual design that we used as a basis for an early interaction model, described in a video prototype. We performed a heuristic evaluation of the video prototype to refine our interaction model with a focus on usability issues. With a new interaction model for the Tangible Keyboard, we performed a Wizard of Oz study for a specific application of the Tangible Keyboard that we call Silly Poems.

1) Metaphorical Design

The computer keyboard is a familiar object that is used to input letters, numbers, and other symbols by clicking or pressing keys, after which the symbol is either displayed on a computer screen or causes the state of the application and/or the computer screen to change in some way. Each key on a computer keyboard is labeled with an alphanumeric or special symbol, indicating what data is entered when striking that key. The use of a keyboard is pervasive to computer input and therefore has significant value for being familiar. We designed the Tangible Keyboard as an alternative to the keyboard for creative composition, not that it replaces the keyboard as the default interaction design. The keyboard is a productivity tool, and the Tangible Keyboard is a creativity support tool. In designing new tangible input devices, there is a lot to be gained from being similar to, but different from, the established keyboard device. The tangible cubes as keys can be arranged as movable objects into various adjacencies providing visual feedback for further recognition and additional functions for their composition. Tangible interaction with the cubes comprises a variety of different actions such as press, shake, neighbor, and flip. These actions serve as the user input to the software running on the cubes. For example, one affordance that is shared by the traditional keyboard and the Tangible Keyboard is the action of pressing down on the key to affect a change in the state of the application or on the display. Interaction goes beyond the physical surface since keys can be picked up and manipulated in the air.

To re-conceptualize the traditional keyboard, we identified two features that are transferred to our design: Symbols and Keys[1]. Symbols: The alphabet of keyboard letters is analogous to an open set of symbols on our tangible cubes. Keys: The fixed arrangement of QWERTY key button-like objects is analogous to freely arrangeable tangible digital objects. We describe aspects of Symbols and Keys that are relevant to our design of the Tangible Keyboard and provide a summary in Tables 3.1 and 3.2.

---

[1] We acknowledge Alberto Gonzalez and Tim Clausner for the development of the metaphorical design concepts.

Table 3.1: Comparison of features between the QWERTY keyboard and the Tangible Keyboard

Features of Keys	Keyboard	Tangible Keyboard
Symbol on key	Letter	Word, image, etc.
Key object	Finger-sized button	Graspable cubes
User action	Press	Hold, arrange, press, flip, shake
Layout of keys	Fixed arrangement	Variable arrangement

Table 3.2: Comparison of I/O properties between the QWERTY keyboard and the Tangible Keyboard

I/O Properties	Keyboard	Tangible Keyboard
Cross-device interaction	Keyboard, mouse, and computer	Cubes and tablet
Space-multiplexed input	Yes, but fixed keyboard	Yes
Space-multiplexed output	No	Yes
Multimodal output	No	Display screen and audio
Scales to large symbol sets	No	Yes, but limited by number of cubes
Assign symbol	None	Challenging

Symbols. Labels on a keyboard are alphabets in the broad sense. They consist of the set of letter symbols used for writing alphabetic languages or of the phonetic symbols in some Asian languages used for writing in addition to characters (e.g., Hangul in Korean, Kana in Japanese, and Pinyin in Chinese). We re-conceptualize the labels on keys of the QWERTY keyboard, such that labels are no longer limited to letters of an alphabet, numbers, and special symbols. Symbols on the Tangible Keyboard are unlimited, including words, characters, phrases, notes, sounds, images, icons, and other symbolic categories.

Keys. The keys on a keyboard are the physical instruments that allow the user to enter data through pressing one or more physical objects. A keyboard describes a collection of keys. For example, pressing down on a key of the QWERTY keyboard actuates its function. While the QWERTY keys don't change in physical appearance, the keys themselves have numerous uses. For example, the "S" key is labeled with only the letter "S" visibly inscribed on the button, but it affords more general functions:

- Type a lower case "s" (although the default letter typed is lowercase, the key is labeled uppercase);

- Type an upper case "S" (with SHIFT key);

- Save the current file (with CTRL key);

- Play a music note (D) in Garage Band or Logic Pro;

- Move down or back in some video games; and

- Perform other application or user defined actions.

While the keyboard affords a wide range of options for data input, there are limitations, particularly for creative composition:

- Visual content on the face of the keys is fixed.

- Additional functionality offered by the keys (e.g., shortcuts) requires recall rather than recognition.

- Arrangement of the keys is fixed.

- Interaction is confined to a planar surface.

We address these limitations in the Tangible Keyboard by transforming the concept of a keyboard from a focus on selecting letters to form words to a focus on assembling objects (e.g., words, pictures, etc.) to form creative compositions. The limitations are addressed in the following ways:

- Symbols are displayed on the face of a cube, enabling its symbolic content to vary.

- The functionality of the keys is based on recognition rather than recall.

- Keys can be arranged as movable objects into various adjacencies providing visual feedback for further recognition and additional functions for information retrieval or composition.

- Interaction goes beyond the physical surface since keys can be picked up and manipulated in the air.

Touch-typing and symbol assignment are two aspects of the traditional keyboard that do not transfer to the Tangible Keyboard. The closed set of keyboard letters and fixed key arrangement enables mastery of touch-typing skill not afforded by the Tangible Keyboard. The traditional keyboard does not require the user to assign letters to keys, but scaling large open sets of symbols to the Tangible Keyboard keys is limited by the number of keys. For example, how to input a word or picture and assign it to a key poses an interaction challenge. Table 3.2 notes this gap in the keyboard metaphor.

2) Heuristic Evaluation

Heuristic evaluation is a usability inspection method for finding the usability problems in a UI design, as described by Nielsen and Molich (1990). Heuristic evaluation involves having a small set of evaluators evaluate the interface: In our case, the design team served as the evaluators. The evaluators judge its compliance with recognized usability principles and identify issues with the design. In our case, we performed the evaluation over short period of time to identify the most obvious issues.

Nielsen (1994) developed categorical heuristics to identify usability problems in HCI design and Norman (2005) described design principles, as shown in Table 3.3. Some of Norman's principles are similar in concept to Nielsen's heuristics, and others are more specialized in particular areas. For instance, affordance and mapping can be more specialized for physical action in terms of dealing with tangible devices. Nevertheless, Norman's design principles were not developed with tangible and touchable interaction models in mind.

Table 3.3: Nielsen's and Norman's design heuristics	
Nielsen's Heuristics	**Norman's Heuristics**
Visibility of system status.	Consistency
Match between system and real world.	Visibility
User control and freedom.	Affordance
Consistency and standards.	Mapping
Error prevention.	Constraints
Recognition rather than recall.	Feedback
Flexibility and efficiency of use.	
Aesthetic and minimalist design.	
Help users recognize, diagnose, and recover from errors.	
Help and documentation	

We specifically applied Nielsen's heuristics to evaluate the initial design for the Tangible Keyboard, even though they were developed for desktop applications. We implicitly considered Norman's principles, but did not specifically refer to them in our analysis. While Nielsen's heuristics do not reflect the physical features of tangible interaction, their application can highlight how we can adapt the heuristics for tangible interaction design.

We investigated the affordances of the Tangible Keyboard tablet and cubes by creating a mock-up of the user experience in the Pattern Maker application as a video[2] using simulated tablet and cubes displays along with user actions and system actions. Six annotators applied heuristics by annotating the video with comments. All annotations were coded according to heuristic category

---

[2]   http://maryloumaher.net/DInKs/videos/DinksVideoPrototype.mp4.

(Nielsens'), device type (cube, tablet), interaction type (visual, manual interaction), and issue type (positive, negative).

Table 3.4[3] reports the percent total of 68 comments in each heuristic category derived from the video annotations (the table does not sum to 100% due to rounding). A majority of comments are related to cubes interaction (63%), such that more than half of all comments (54%) centered on cubes interaction in heuristic categories: Consistency (35%) and Match between system and real world (19%). Each cell of the table includes both positive and negative comments, because while 73% of all comments were negative and 24% were positive, comment polarity did not differentiate the types. Specifically, comments about consistency included, in principle, both positive remarks (consistent) and negative remarks (inconsistent). For example, consistent and inconsistent uses of the Neighbor action on cubes helped us to revise the design of this action. The Match heuristic also, in principle, evoked both positive and negative remarks.

Only those heuristics that received at least one comment were included in Table 3.4. The heuristics Visibility of Systems Status, User Control, and Flexibility and Efficiency of use received relatively few comments. On average annotators made 12.2 comments, ranging between 40 and 2 comments. Few or no comments in a category may have reflected variable expertise among some annotators, which included HCI, design, and cognitive science. Even so, we believe that the categories that received the majority of comments did so overall because these represented overwhelming salience or importance relative to other categories. For example, user control is of little importance if inconsistencies in affordances are highly salient.

Table 3.4: Summary of heuristic evaluation: percent of total (n=68) comments					
Heuristic	**Visual Design**		**Interaction Design**		
	Cubes	Tablet	Cubes	Tablet	Total
Visibility of System Status	3%	10%	7%	1%	31%
Match between System and Real World	1%	3%	19%	3%	26%
Consistency	1%	1%	35%	9%	38%
User Control	0%	0%	0%	1%	1%
Flexibility and Efficiency of Use	0%	0%	1%	1%	3%
TOTAL	6%	15%	63%	16%	

The most common comments resulting from the heuristic evaluation are about cube actions, specific to two heuristics: interaction inconsistency, where some user actions on cubes caused inconsistent system actions, and system/world mismatch, where some user actions on

---

[3]   We acknowledge Tim Clausner for performing this analysis of our heuristic evaluation data.

cubes did not match how real physical objects behave or mismatch common user mental models. In response to our heuristic evaluation, we made five changes to the interaction model:

- **Press (Single Cube).** This action had a negative feedback in the heuristic "match between system and real world." Pressing a single cube is a changing function in the previous design that changes selected shape, color, and scale on a cube. However, Press is used as a selecting or fixing function. Thus, this action was changed to Drag. Drag is a more natural action than Press in this case, since Drag is more consistent with the commonly used function of moving to the next screen when people use a smart phone or tablet.

- **Neighbor (Shape Cube + Empty Cube).** The neighboring mapping also had an issue regarding "match between system and real world." The heuristic evaluation pointed out that the neighboring action is not appropriate in this case. Thus, the Neighbor action was changed to Neighbor + Pour (Tilt), since the Pour action was a good match in terms of putting an object into another container.

- **Neighbor + Tilt (Shape Cube + Scale Cube).** The scale cube is a numeric symbol, and this action used the combination of a shape cube and scale cube vertically. This is not a good match between system and real world. After getting feedback from the heuristic evaluation, we changed the action to Neighbor since it looks like a math equation when the shape cube neighbors a scale cube.

- **Neighbor + Shake (Shape cube + Shape cube).** The heuristic evaluation mentioned that this action has problems similar to Neighbor (Shape Cube + Empty Cube) in terms of putting an object into another container. Thus, we applied the same action with Neighbor (Shape Cube + Empty Cube) which is the Neighbor + Pour (Tilt). Moreover, applying the same action for similar purposes increases consistency in the overall design.

- **Neighbor + Shake (Color cube + Color cube).** Although this action had a positive feedback for the heuristic "match between system and real world," we slightly changed this action. The previous shaking action involves a horizontal combination of cubes. However, paint is liquid in the real world and therefore effected by gravity. So, we changed the horizontal combination of cubes to a vertical combination of cubes for a more natural affordance.

3) Wizard of Oz Study

Our Wizard of Oz study[4] was performed on a partially implemented application called Silly Poems. Silly Poems is a prototype application for creating limericks. A limerick has five lines, each with a specific number of syllables and a particular rhyming scheme. In our application, the tablet displays the limerick composition in progress while the Sifteo cubes™ (i.e., the keys) each display a word and the number of syllables that word will add to the limerick. We asked an amateur poet to use six cubes to create a limerick using the Think Aloud (Boren and Ramey, 2000) and Wizard of Oz methods, illustrated in Figure 3.5. After completing her poem, shown in Figure 3.6, we conducted a semi-structured interview with the participant.

Figure 3.5: Wizard of Oz Study: expanding the visual and interaction capabilities of the Tangible Keyboard using Post-It® Notes.

The participant was told that the cubes could perform the following actions: display a new randomly selected word when shaken, change the word to an image or sound when pressed, and add the words on the cubes to a selected line of the limerick when flipped. Instead of a tablet displaying the composition, the experimenter wrote the words on a white board wall in front of the participant each time the participant flipped a cube. When the participant requested a word that was not in the library, the experimenter would write the word on a sticky note and place the note on top of a cube. When the participant wanted to modify a line or word from the composition, the experimenter would also write out the words on sticky notes. The Wizard of Oz method provided a flexible environment for creative composition that empowered the participant to change and explore the design space of interaction possibilities.

---

[4] We acknowledge Alberto Gonzalez and Katy Gero for performing the Wizard of Oz.

1. There once was a bike that cried wolf

2. A muzzle appear with a poof

3. She pedaled all day

4. Til her chain became grey

5. But still her call was a "woof"

Figure 3.6: Limerick created in the study (transcribed from the white board for legibility).

The participant made the following suggestions for the interaction design for Silly Poems.

- **Retrieving new words.** The participant was told that shaking a cube could retrieve a new random word, but the participant wanted to retrieve certain kinds of words. For example, retrieving a word that rhymes with one already in the limerick was important. The participant suggested that selecting a word from the composition (i.e., tablet) should move that word onto a cube, and then placing a second cube above or below that cube would generate a rhyming word. She associated placing a cube before or after another cube as indicating the sequence of words in the poem, and above or below as alternative words related to a word in the poem.

- **Rearranging the words on a line.** The participant suggested that selecting a line number on the composition could put all the words in that line onto the cubes. During the interview, the participant commented on how this let her rearrange the words in a way that isn't well supported in keyboard/mouse or touch applications.

- **Adding words to the limerick.** The participant was told that flipping one or more cubes would replace the currently selected line on the tablet with the words on the cube. After creating an initial limerick, the participant wanted only to change one portion of a line. The experimenter suggested sections of text could be selected, and then flipping the cubes would replace the selected words. This allowed the participant to more thoroughly explore the design space using all the cubes, otherwise they would have to reserve some cubes for the parts (i.e., words) of the line they weren't planning to change.

- **Creating word phrases.** The participant suggested that bumping two cubes together could combine smaller words onto one cube. This is useful when there are not enough cubes to display or compose an entire line of the limerick. It could also be useful to de-clutter the exploration by pairing minor parts of speech (i.e., prepositions, articles).

Additional suggestions from the post-interview include:

- Provide as many cubes as there can be words in a line of the poem so the user can flip the entire poem line.

- Show a definition or word etymology when a cube is pressed. This is an alternative to the press action providing the same word in a different media (e.g., image), and instead it provides the meaning of the word.

- Generate new words by putting letters on each of the cubes and using word completion algorithms whenever letters are neighbored with adjacent cubes.

- Display a new word on a cube using speech recognition.

- See alternative rhyming words when cubes are neighbored top and bottom. Finding all possible rhyming words is important when there are only a limited number. When there are many rhyming words, show words that are surprising.

During the final part of the interview, the participant was asked where the Tangible Keyboard could be helpful in the writing process and where it could be limiting. Here is a summary of her main points:

- Interacting with the Tangible Keyboard could be slow during periods of inspiration where many ideas are being generated and a keyboard would better support quickly jotting down different ideas.

- The Tangible Keyboards could be most helpful when rearranging words in a line of a poem, when searching for related words or words that rhyme, or for generating inspiration for new ideas by displaying words you hadn't previously thought about using.

Throughout the task and interview, the participant offered many comparisons between the Tangible Keyboard and classic keyboard interaction. The participant stated that she normally writes poetry using pen and paper or using the keyboard with a plain-text editor on a computer. In the interview, the participant made remarks about what types of interaction were possible using digital interactive keys (DInKs) that were not possible (or involved "obnoxious switching" between applications) using keyboard interfaces. Her description of the interaction included the phrases: visualizing things, rearranging words, showing relevant words, displaying definitions, pulling words down from the tablet, etc.

3.1.5 INTERACTION MODEL

The Tangible Keyboard interaction model presented here is our latest version of the model and is expressed with the Pattern Maker application, illustrated in Figure 3.7, to facilitate understanding of the model. The moel is described in two parts: the interaction model for the tablet and the interaction model for the cubes.

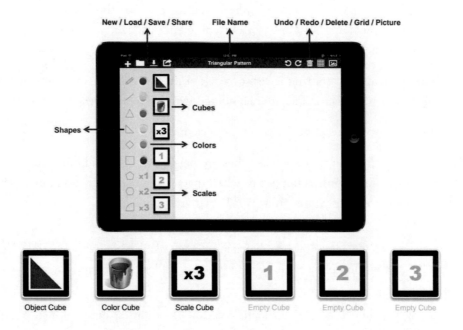

Figure 3.7: Pattern Maker application design using the Tangible Keyboard platform.

The tablet displays a palette and the pattern design as the user composes it. The palette consists of shapes, colors, scales, and icons that can be transferred to activated cubes. Users can assign shape, color, or scale to a particular cube by dragging items from the palette to a cube icon. Once the user assigns a shape, color, or scale to several cubes, the user can create compositions using neighboring, pouring, shaking, and pressing on the cubes. Users can explore changing a selected shape on the cube by tilting or shaking the different types of cubes with neighboring to create new shapes. They can also neighbor cubes together to change a shape's color or scale. For instance, if the user neighbors a yellow paint cube with a black triangle cube and then pours the color onto the triangle, the triangle color will be changed to yellow. The user can change the size of the shape by neighboring the shape cube with a scale cube. The user can make a new color by shaking two color cubes together, or make a new shape by shaking two shapes together. Additionally, the user can modify the composition on the canvas. For example, the user can delete a shape by dragging the shape to the trash icon. Thus, the tablet and cubes have complementary roles for composing a pattern. While Figure 3.7 illustrates the interaction, Table 3.5 shows the interaction model that maps a user action to a system action specifically in the context of the Pattern Maker app rather than a generic design for the Tangible Keyboard. This interaction model went through much iteration with a focus on consistency, usability, discoverability, and learnability.

Table 3.5: Interaction model for the Pattern Maker app of Tangible Keyboard		
User Action	**Illustrated User Action**	**System Action**
Press (Single Cube)		Move to next shape, color, or scale on cube
Neighbor (Shape Cube + Empty Cube)		Copy and add shape to another shape cube
Neighbor + Tilt (Shape Cube + Color Cube)		Change color or shape
Neighbor + Tilt (Shape Cube + Scale Cube)		Modify shape by multiplying by a scale
Neighbor + shake (Color cube + Color cube)		Mixing one color with another color

Neighbor + Shake (Shape cube + Shape cube)		Combine both shapes on one cube
Shake (Shape Cube)		Select a random shape, color, or scale on cube
Flip (Shape Cube)		Mirror Shape
Neighbor + Press (Shape cube + Shape cube)		Move combined shape from cubes to tablet
Neighbor (Shape Cube + Shape Cube)		Arrange shapes for creative composition

3.1.6 DESIGN HEURISTICS

The design of interaction models for TUI has yet to take into account a common set of heuristics to develop consistency across applications. We have iteratively developed a set of heuristics that are specific to the design space of TUIs that serve as guidelines for future designs.

Visibility of system status. The display on the tangible devices should provide visual feedback to the user that they are powered on and their current state as an object or control cube.

Match between the digital and the physical world. The actions on the tangible devices should result in visual or interactive changes that match the effect of similar actions in the physical world.

User control and freedom. Users should be able to control what they see on the tangible devices and be able to change that as needed.

Consistency and standards. Each action on a tangible device should have a similar affect in different contexts. Whenever possible, interpret actions in the same way across applications.

Recognition rather than recall. Minimize relying on the user's memory by making objects, actions, and options visible on the tangible devices. The user should not have to look up information from the tablet to understand what they can do on the tangible devices.

Flexibility and efficiency of use. Allow different ways to achieve the same goal: The user should be able to perform some actions on either the tablet or on the tangible device.

Aesthetic and minimalist design. Use the minimal display space on small tangible devices efficiently: Keep the visual design simple and clear.

Easy-to-discover tangible interaction. The way in which the user moves tangibles to do certain input actions should be discoverable, easy to do, and consistent since the system uses a new kind of input device.

Minimum physical strain. When the interactive system requires various physical actions between touching a tablet display and moving tangible devices, the design should minimize physical strain and use each device for complementary tasks.

3.2   DESIGNING TANGIBLE MODELS

3.2.1   CONTEXT OF USE

The context of use for the design of Tangible Models is architectural design, with a focus on configuration design using a library of 3D objects. The configuration task includes a scene or architectural context, and a library of 3D models that are the elements of the configuration. An example of a configuration task is the layout of the 3D objects in a room design. The scene is a visualization of the room as a floor plan and as a 3D perspective, showing doors, walls, windows, and other relevant features such as stairs or elevators. The 3D objects are digital models of furniture and other contents of a room. Traditionally, this task is achieved using sketching on paper, or using a CAD system on a desktop with a keyboard and mouse.

The context of use for Tangible Models is also to design a collaborative design environment. Often a design environment favors a single designer using a single display and input device. Collaboration in such an environment is supported by sharing the input device and negotiating turn taking. The Tangible Models design supports collaboration by providing multiple input devices placed on a shared tabletop display. These space-multiplexed input devices support synchronization during collaboration as a simultaneous process of modifying the design rather than a sequential process of turn taking.

3.2.2   DESIGN GOALS

The primary design goal for Tangible Models design was to create a new way for users to manipulate 3D models by grasping rather than by pointing. Rather than design a new computer-aided design application, the goal of Tangible Models is to provide a new interaction design for any existing CAD application. The effect of introducing space-multiplexed input devices is a new way to support collaborative design. In summary, the design goals are:

- a tangible interaction with 3D models,

- a new interaction design for existing CAD systems, and

- a new approach to supporting synchronized collaboration.

3.2.3 TECHNOLOGY SELECTION

1) CAD Application

Tangible Models was developed as an alternative input device to the ArchiCAD application. Archi-CAD users can create a virtual building by selecting, scaling, and locating structural and architectural elements like walls, slabs, roofs, doors, windows, and furniture. The ArchiCAD library includes a variety of pre-designed, customizable 3D models of these elements. While, theoretically, any CAD system could have been selected, at the time, ArchiCAD provided the APIs to integrate the new input devices to existing functions. With the traditional keyboard and mouse interface, the user has time-multiplexed interaction. With Tangible Models, the user has space-multiplexed interaction.

2) Tangible Blocks with ARToolKit

Simple blocks are used to represent 3D models from the CAD library. The ARToolkit was selected as the software platform for this interaction design: Each block displays a marker, and the visualization of the associated 3D model is superimposed on the marker in the visual display. In this implementation, we used a shared vertical display rather than individual see-through head-mounted displays. Figure 3.8(a) shows a block with a marker for a specific model of a table. Figure 3.8(b) show the superposition of a 3D shelf object on a block. Figure 3.8(c) shows a scene with several blocks, each with their associated 3D model superimposed in the visual display. Multiple 3D blocks allow multi-users to concurrently select, place, and relocate pieces on the tabletop using two hands. When users manipulate multiple blocks, each block allows direct control of virtual objects while communicating digital information visually to the user. Through the 3D blocks, the users also gain tactile feedback from their interaction. ARToolKit is used for developing AR application and augmenting the 3D visual outputs of the design on the vertical display through a camera sensing device. ARToolKit allows editing the virtual model in a 3D view, and navigating in real time to check the design.

(a) (b) (c)

Figure 3.8: (a) 3D block with a pattern, (b) shelf panel virtual model, and (c) 3D multiple blocks.

3) Tabletop Computer and Vertical Display Devices

The tabletop display is the platform on which the tangible input and output devices are located, providing a 2D projection of the 3D scene as the location in which tangible interaction takes place (see Figure 3.9). The vertical display device includes a camera that provides the image of the scene used by the ARToolkit to identify markers on the blocks and locate the blocks in the 3D scene. This combined tabletop and vertical display system design is based on two principles for improving the 3D design experience: the use of a horizontal projection surface with tangible input devices; and a vertical screen for interacting with a perspective visualization of the 3D design. We chose not to use a heads-up device because, at the time, these devices were expensive and hard to use. We expect that the vertical display may be replaced with see-through augmented reality glasses in similar interaction design models.

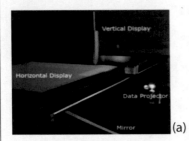

Figure 3.9: Tabletop system: (a) horizontal table, (b) vertical screen, and (c) 3D blocks.

3.2.4 DESIGN METHODS

The design method we describe here is an analytical approach to understanding the cognitive affects of Tangible Models. We performed an empirical study to compare the Tangible Models interaction design (TUI) with the traditional keyboard and mouse interaction design (GUI). Rather than using subjective self-reports such as questionnaires and comments, we measured the participants' cognitive actions using a protocol analysis in order to analyze their actual design behavior rather than the participants' perceived design behavior. The methodology comprises five steps: protocol data collection, protocol segmentation, coding of segments, analysis of codes, and interpretation (Foreman and Gillett 1997; Gero and Tang 2001). More detail about this study is available in Kim and Maher (2008)[5].

- **Protocol data collection.** A protocol is the recorded behavior of the participants, which in this study is a video of the participants while engaging in a design task. Nine designers were observed in a within-subjects experiment design: each designer

---

[5]   We acknowledge Mi Jeong Kim for setting up the conditions and performing the protocol analysis.

performed a design task similar in complexity in each condition: GUI and TUI. They were asked to report as continuously as possible what they were thinking as they carried out the design tasks for about 20 minutes. Table 3.6 describes the similarities and differences between the two conditions.

Table 3.6: Outline of the experiment sessions (Kim and Maher, 2008)		
	TUI Condition	**GUI Condition**
Interface/Application	3D blocks/ARToolKit	Mouse and keyboard/ArchiCAD
Hardware	Tabletop and webcam/LCD screen	Desktop/LCD screen
Training/Design Session	5-10 min/20 min	5-10 min/20 min
Designer	Individual 2nd or 3rd architecture student	
Design Tasks	Home office or design office renovation	

- **Protocol segmentation.** The protocol was segmented according to speaker; that is, when the speaker changed, a new segment occurred. The statements were further segmented along the lines of designer's intentions or changes in their actions.

- **Coding scheme.** A coding scheme was developed to measure the difference between the traditional keyboard and mouse interaction and the Tangible Models interaction. The coding scheme had three groups of codes:

  ○ HCI: Actions related to interaction with the CAD models.

  ○ Designer: Perceptions and cognitive issues expressed verbally by the participant.

  ○ Design process: Statements that reveal the participant's stage and progression in a design process model.

The coding scheme comprised six categories. 3D modeling and gesture actions at the HCI level, perceptual and functional actions at the designer level, and set-up goal actions and co-evolution issues at the design process level.

The HCI codes consist of 3D modeling and gesture actions as listed in Table 3.7, which represent designers' interaction with the external representation. These physical actions are motor activities produced in using the interface and are a sensory support for designers' spatial cognition. The 3D modeling action category represents the summary of operations on external representations, describing the "movement" of 3D furniture objects and the "inspection" of external representations and design briefs. This coding scheme is associated with a designer's perceptual actions. The gesture action category represents a designer's movement other than 3D modeling actions.

Table 3.7: HCI action codes (Kim and Maher, 2007)	
3D Modeling Actions	**Description**
PlaceNew	Place a new object on the plan from the library
PlaceExisting	Change the location of an initially given object for the first time
ReplaceExisting	Change the location of an existing object again
Rotate	Change the orientation of an existing object only
Remove	Delete/remove an existing object
Library	Search for an object in the library
InspectBrief	Inspect the design brief
InspectScreen	Inspect layout on the vertical screen
InspectTable	Inspect layout on the horizontal table
Gesture Actions	**Description**
Design gesture	Large hand movement above the 3D plan on the screen or table
General gesture	General speech-accompanying hand gesture
Touch gesture	Touch a 3D block with hands or the mouse
Modeling action	No gesture while modeling

The designer level consists of perceptual and functional actions as listed in Table 3.8, which represent how designers perceive visuo-spatial features from the external representation and reason about functional issues from the perceived information. The visuo-spatial features are the cues for the reasoning actions. These two cognitive action categories directly related to designers' spatial cognition will help in identifying possible differences between the two interface environments, by showing either an increase or a decrease in levels of attention to visuo-spatial features and in conceiving of functional issues. Perceptual actions coding scheme is used to investigate as a measure of designers' perceptive abilities for spatial knowledge. The perception of the form and spatial relationships of design objects is the main component of measuring designers' perceptual actions. Functional actions refer to reasoning actions of conceiving functional meanings that are associated with visuo-spatial features.

Table 3.8: Designer perception and function codes (Kim and Maher, 2007)

Perceptual Actions	Description
E-visual feature	Attention to a visual feature (geometric or physical properties) of an element
E-relation	Attention to a spatial relationship among elements or orientation of an element
E-space	Attention to a location of a space
E-object	Attention to a location of an object
N-relation	Creation of a new spatial relationship (local and global) among elements
N-space	Creation of new space among elements
D-visual feature	Discovery of a visual feature of an element
D-relation	Discovery of a spatial relationship among elements
D-space	Discovery of an implicit space between elements
Functional Actions	**Description**
F-circulation	Think of circulation: behavioral sense
F-view	Think of view: visionary sense
F-furniture	Think of function of furniture: concrete function
F-abstract	Think of function of areas: abstract function

The design process level consists of set-up goal actions and co-evolution as listed in Table 3.9, which represent designers' "problem-finding" behaviors associated with creative design. The reason for investigating the problem-finding behaviors is that designers re-formulated the design problem in response to visuo-spatial reasoning, and such problem-finding behaviors strongly reflect the creative aspect of design processes. Set-up goal actions refer to conceptual actions of introducing functional issues as new design requirements that restructure the design problem. The co-evolution category consists of the problem space and the solution space, representing the two design spaces designers explore iteratively while designing.

Table 3.9: Design process codes (Kim and Maher, 2007)

Set-up Goal Actions	Description
G-knowledge	Goals to introduce new functions derived from explicit knowledge or experience
G-previous	Goals to introduce new functions extended from a previous goal
G-implicit	Goals to introduce new functions in a way that is implicit
G-brief	Goals to introduce new functions based on the given list of initial requirements
G-repeat	Repeated goals from a previous segment
Co-evolution	**Description**
P-space	The features and constraints required for a design solution
S-space	The features and behaviors of a design solution

- **Analysis of codes.** A detailed analysis is published in Kim and Maher (2008). Here we provide the highlights of the analysis.

  Compared to the GUI condition, designers using TUI exhibited the following patterns of behavior:

  - frequent 3D modeling actions possibly reducing cognitive load on user interface,

  - more focus-shifts in design thinking through frequent 3D modeling actions,

  - frequent "revisited" 3D modeling actions resulting in multiple representations, and

  - perceptual ability for creating and perceiving new visuo-spatial features through frequent "revisited" 3D modeling actions.

  Compared with the GUI condition, designers using TUI exhibited the following patterns of behavior:

  - more gestures, specifically more "design" and "general" gestures leading to whole-body interaction with the external representation using hands and arms, and

  - perceptual ability for existing visuo-spatial features through "design" and "touch" gestures.

  The analysis showed that the TUI produced epistemic actions revealing information that is hard to compute mentally. Rather than "internalizing" the moves of the 3D objects, the designers performed more 3D modeling actions as epistemic actions, which may reflect a reduction of designers' cognitive load. Through the "revisited" 3D modeling actions, designers produced more multiple representations, resulting in revision of the design ideas. Consequently, designers in the TUI condition changed the external world through the 3D modeling actions, allowing them to offload their thought, thereby supporting further perceptual activities.

Furthermore, they exhibited more immersive gestures using large hand movements, which functioned as a complementary strategy to the 3D modeling actions in assisting in designers' perception. The immersive interactions produced by the "design" gestures might be associated with designers' spatial cognition since they support designers' cognitive process in designing. "Touch" gestures played the role of "organizing activities" that recruit external elements to reduce cognitive loads. They did not produce direct changes to the external representation, but stimulated designers' perceptual activities.

Compared with the GUI condition, designers exhibited the following patterns of behavior in the TUI condition:

° more perceptual activities;

° more new visuo-spatial features were created, perceived, and discovered; and

° greater focus on spatial relations among elements.

Compared with the GUI condition, designers exhibited the following patterns of behavior in the TUI condition:

° more new functional issues as design requirements were introduced, specifically in an implicit way or by retrieving explicit knowledge or experience;

° more transitions between the "problem" and "solution" spaces were produced; and

° more time was spent reasoning about the design problem.

- **Interpretation.** The results reveal that designers using Tangible Models spent more time reformulating the design problem by introducing new functional issues as design requirements. The designers developed the design problem and alternative ideas for a solution more pervasively, progressing in a co-evolutionary process. Their problem-finding behaviors were clearly increased during the use of the Tangible Models. In addition, unexpected discoveries via their perceptual and "revisited" 3D modeling actions were considered for examining the process of re-representation. The high instances of the combined code "discovery" suggest that the "revisited" 3D modeling actions resulted in the production of multiple representations that enabled designers to discover new visuo-spatial features, and afforded them more opportunities to gain the sudden insight to find key concepts for a creative design.

3.2.5   INTERACTION MODEL

In the Tangible Models design, the tangible blocks did not include sensors that recorded or responded to their movement. So, when considering how to describe the interaction model, we observed the role of hand movements or gestures while the designers were using the blocks to perform the configuration task. The designers performed actions on the blocks that effectively changed the digital representation of the design. Therefore, one kind of interaction is the "movement" of 3D objects and the "inspection" of the digital representation. While thinking and talking about the design task, the designers employed gestures other than moving the blocks. We observed these different types of actions and gestures:

- Actions included movement of 3D blocks representing 3D models.

- Design gestures occur when a designer describes his/her ideas simultaneously with large hand-movements over the plan.

- General gestures occur when a designer simply moves his/her hands without a specific design intention.

- Touch gestures occur when a designer touches multiple 3D blocks using their hands, or digital images using the mouse, which do not accompany any movement change in the design.

3.2.6   DESIGN GUIDELINES

Our design guidelines for the Tangible Models example are derived from the results of our protocol analysis. We have observed consistent differences in the cognitive behavior of the users when engaged with the Tangible Models compared with the traditional keyboard and mouse. We found that the physical interaction with objects in the Tangible Models platform produce epistemic actions as an exploratory activity to assist in designers' spatial cognition. As a design guideline, this implies that the interaction model should have a goal of increasing exploratory actions. We believe that the epistemic 3D modeling actions afforded by the tangible interface resulted in offloading aspects of designers' cognition, and the naturalness of the direct hands-on style of interaction promotes designers' immersion in designing, thus allowing them to perform spatial reasoning more effectively. In addition, designers' perception of visuo-spatial information, especially spatial relations, was improved while using the 3D blocks. The simultaneous generation of new conceptual ideas and perceptual discoveries when attending to the external physical representation may also be explained by a reduction in the cognitive load of holding alternative design configurations in a mental representation. In terms of the design process, we noticed that designers' problem-finding behaviors were increased in parallel with the change in designers' spatial cognition. The problem-finding behaviors and the process of re-representation are cognitive behaviors associated with creative design and therefore should influence the tasks and contexts of use when designing tangible interactive systems.

CHAPTER 4

Gesture-based Interaction

4.1 WHAT IS A GESTURE-BASED INTERACTION?

In this book, we define gesture-based interaction as a human-centric form of interaction wherein the user does not touch a display but interacts with it by performing bodily gestures to interact and communicate with a digital system. A gesture in this context is a coordinated and intended movement of body parts to achieve communication. People use gestures in everyday life to facilitate thinking (Goldin-Meadow, 1999, 2006; Goldin-Meadow and Beilock, 2010; McNeill, 1992; Oviatt, 2006; Namy and Newcombe, 2008), to illustrate communication (Kessell and Tversky, 2006), to send commands to other people (Sclaroff et al., 2005; Song et al., 2011), and more recently to control interactive systems (Müller et al., 2010; Saffer, 2008, Lee et al., 2014; Delamare et al., 2015; Hinrichs et al., 2013). An interactive system that can perceive and respond to the user's gestures could provide a natural and intuitive interface, and be useful in situations where touching or speaking is not possible or convenient. Jetter (2014) claims that gestural input makes computing more natural by enabling communication with a computer the same way we also communicate with one another.

Gesture-based interaction systems are quickly entering public spaces owing to the expansion of low-cost platforms such as Microsoft Kinect (https://developer.microsoft.com/en-us/windows/kinect) and the Leap motion controller device (https://www.leapmotion.com/) that enable gesture-based interaction through mid-air gestures (Cabreira and Hwang, 2015). Mid-air gestures, primarily hand movements, are suited to large screen interaction in places like museums, airports, and public entrances to buildings so that people can view and interact with the content from a distance (Ackad et al., 2014). Even though many public displays have the capabilities to recognize gestures, users seem unwilling to accept gesture-based interactions outside of gaming or novelty applications (Rico et al., 2011). Therefore, designers should carefully consider how to design discoverable gestures for exploring interaction with a public display, how to design systems that recognize the gestures that people perform to control the interactive system, and how the results of this recognition could be presented to engage the user for further interaction.

The goal of this chapter is to introduce the concepts and design issues for gesture-based interaction through two example systems: Gesture Commands and Gesture Dialogue. The Gesture Commands system is gesture-based information system using a large public display to present academic information about courses and faculty at the University of North Carolina Charlotte. The Gesture

Dialogue system (aka *the willful marionette*) is an interactive art installation that encourages a dialogue of gestures between public participants and a 3D scanned human-like machine. Gesture-based interaction includes the design and development of a gesture-recognition system that maps a set of body movements onto a set of recognized gestures. Free-hand gestures that are intended to interact with digital information are unlike TUIs because TUIs require physical manipulation of tangible objects. From a cognitive perspective, gesture interaction lacks the physical affordances of TUIs and therefore presents challenges in the learnability of the interaction model. Users need to draw on existing mental models to discover and remember gestures while interacting with a system.

4.1.1 GESTURE COMMANDS: WALK-UP-AND-USE INFORMATION DISPLAY

We designed a set of gesture commands as a model for a gesture-based interactive information system with large screen displays in public locations that provide information about an institution. This walk-up-and-use information display was developed in the context of a university department and serves as a framework for an interactive display that engages passersby to easily explore various entities and relations about courses and faculty on a public display. The walk-up-and-use information display utilizes gesture recognition via Microsoft Kinect, and is designed so that multiple users may interact with the information system in a public location.

Figure 4.1: Walk-up-and-use information display.

4.1.2 GESTURE DIALOGUE: THE WILLFULL MARIONETTE

Gesture-based interaction can also lead to a new kind of interaction, the evocation of a creative dialogue of gestures between humans and machine. *The willful marionette* is an interactive art installation whose design serves as an example of such a gesture dialogue. The artists' goal in this project is to explore our emotional response to the human body through a gesture-based dialogue between people and a 3D replica of a human body where the dialogue comprises only gesture[6]. The design of the interactive system explored a new kind of gesture-gesture interaction by mapping a set of human gestures to a set of marionette gestures, iteratively creating a dialogue between the participants and the marionette.

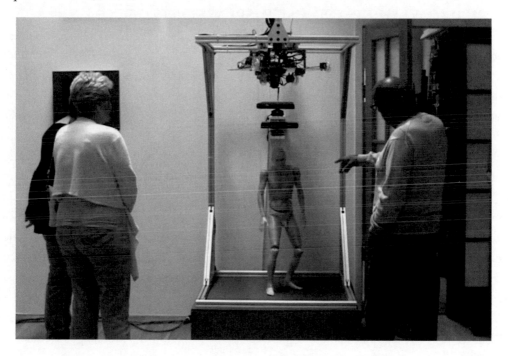

Figure 4.2: *The willful marionette.*

4.2 WHY IS GESTURE-BASED INTERACTION INTERESTING?

Gesture-based interaction has received a lot of attention recently for two major reasons: technology push as the gesture-recognition technology emerging from the games industry has become inexpensive and easy to use; and technology demand as the placement of digital processes in objects

---

[6] We acknowledge Lilla LoCurto and Bill Outcault as the artists that originated and guided the design of *the willful marionette*.

that cannot be tethered to a keyboard and mouse require a new kind of interaction technology and design. The contextual factors that are relevant to gesture-based interaction design are:

1. public walk-up-and-use displays or objects;

2. remote actuators, sensors, and displays;

3. sociable multiple user interaction; and

4. gesture communication.

4.2.1   PUBLIC WALK-UP-AND-USE DISPLAYS OR OBJECTS

Public interactive displays are seen in public spaces such as museums, libraries, airports, plazas, and architectural facades, where they present information and enhance a user's experience in a highly visual and often interactive manner (Motta and Nedel, 2013). Public settings have unique characteristics and therefore unique challenges. Public spaces attract diverse users who differ in age, interests, and levels of experience with technology, and who engage in spontaneous and often unpredictable individual and group activities. In addition, the spatial layout, size, lighting conditions, and social implications of a public setting affects which display technologies and interaction techniques are appropriate and how people will interact with and experience the installation (Hinrichs et al., 2013). A public interactive display presents different requirements and concerns regarding interface design and interaction techniques. Similar to large displays, there are an increasing number of situations in which a user may interact with objects in the home or public places that preclude the standard keyboard and mouse interaction. Such devices include robots, drones, and smart devices. There is a broad range of possibilities in the design for interaction that includes gestures, speech, grasping, and touch. Figure 4.3 illustrates a public walk-up-and-use display that is designed as an engaging game based on physics simulation that motivates passersby to interact with it. (Walter et al. 2013). StrikeAPose is an installation of public displays that show mirror-image reactions to the gestures of the audience and to play with virtual cubes.

Figure 4.3: Public walk-up-and-use display: StrikeAPose. Used with permission (Walter et al. 2013).

1) Walk-Up-and-Use Information Display

With the advent of affordable large display screens, university buildings are hosting large displays within hallways and vestibules to serve as electronic bulletin boards running a slideshow of information. We designed a walk-up-and-use information display to explore the design issues in the context of students on campus. Instead of having static bulletin boards, this system provides an interactive user-driven approach to exploring campus information. In order to use the system, the user needs to discover which gestures cause different information to be displayed. This kind of interaction design has a focus on being consistent, easily discovered, and easy to learn.

2) *The Willful Marionette*

While *the willful marionette* is also a public walk-up-and-use system, there is no intention to create an interaction model that is easily learned in order for interaction to be effective. The people interacting with *the willful marionette* are more appropriately referred to as participants rather than users. As passersby notice *the willful marionette*, they may choose to come into range of the marionette. The marionette will respond to the "approach" gesture by turning to face the participant. Through this initial engagement, the participant is encouraged to do more gestures, only to discover that *the willful marionette* responds with his own gestures rather than mimics the gestures of the participants. This effectively results in a gesture dialogue. This kind of interaction design has a focus on being engaging and personal.

4.2.2   REMOTE ACTUATORS, SENSORS, AND DISPLAYS

Remote actuators and sensors allow people to interact at a distance and without props. This so-called mid-air interaction has received a lot of attention as an interaction modality for public displays and objects. Mid-air interactions allow ample room for creativity, giving designers a variety of options in designing the interactions. Mid-air interaction systems receive visual input and recognize users' gestures without requiring them to touch keys or screens. Mid-air gestures make public displays more attractive to passersby and get them easily and actively engaged with them in a public setting. Moreover, users do not have to make detours to approach the displays. Because the displays work without touch, they have decreased hygienic risks that may affect touch-based systems. Therefore, we expect to see more gesture-based interactive displays in public spaces.

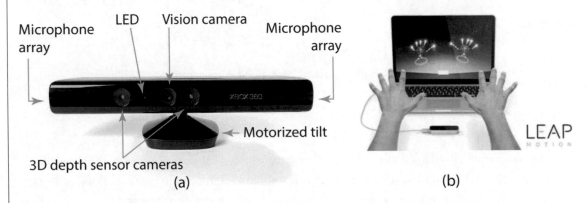

Figure 4.4: (a) Microsoft Kinect (courtesy of iStock.com/kursatunsal); (b) Leap Motion (courtesy of Leap Motion).

The two most common devices today for sensing human motion for gesture recognition are Microsoft Kinect and Leap Motion Controller, illustrated in Figure 4.4. Based on these devices, we are seeing that gesture-based interaction has focused on a pre-designed set of gestures like swipe, wave, and point (Liu et al., 2005; Tang, 2011). Automatic recognition of gestures from whole-body movement is a challenge for gesture interaction since different people naturally move in diverse ways when expressing a swipe, move, or point (Yang et al., 2007). Many previous studies on action recognition have concentrated on using 2D videos (Li et al., 2008; Pollard et al., 2002) or still images. However, those approaches are limited to expressing lateral motion only. Recently, 3D body joint locations have been widely used in human action-recognition tasks (Li et al., 2010; Raptis et al., 2011; Sung et al., 2012) because the Kinect provides an easily accessible and affordable depth camera and more explicit information for describing human movement (Jenkins et al., 2007; Liu et al., 2012; Mullaney et al., 2014). Various interfaces (Triesch and Von Der Malsburg, 1998; Waldherr et al., 2000) have been developed to track a person and recognize gestures. The mapping of gestures to input commands (Hoffmann, 1996; Yamane et al., 2004) enables the interactive devices to track and respond to a specific set of the users' movements.

1) Walk-Up-and-Use Information Display

The walk-up-and-use information display system uses the Microsoft Kinect technology to recognize gestures based on the relative movement of the skeleton of the user. The system recognizes one person at a time, providing visual feedback on the display to indicate which person and which hand the system is tracking. The interaction design includes the recognition of a gesture for selection, in which the interpretation of the meaning of selection depends on the context of the location on the display. Selection can result either in enlarging the item being selected or initiating the presentation of more detailed information about the item being selected. The simplicity of the gesture-recognition process assures that the interaction is consistent and easy to discover.

2) *The Willful Marionette*

The willful marionette also uses the Microsoft Kinect technology to recognize gestures. This interaction design allows for the recognition of several gestures, such as wave, approach, and bend over, and is able to track two participants. The recognized participant-gesture pair is sent to a Puppet Master application that maps the human gesture to a puppet gesture response. The command for the marionette to perform is sent to an Arduino application that controls the movement of strings that move the body parts of the marionette. The mapping from the participant gesture to the marionette gesture is based on a gesture dialogue table that associates a set of marionette gestures with each human gesture, and the selection of which gesture in the set to perform is random. This gesture dialogue design is intended to engage the participant with the recognition of many human gestures, and the pattern of marionette responses is not predictable; and therefore, the participant continues to interact in order to discover a pattern in the interaction.

4.2.3   SOCIABLE MULTIPLE-USER INTERACTION

Public displays can be very effective by creating a sociable multiple-user interaction; this is known as the honey-pot effect (Michelis and Müller, 2011). Gesture-based interactive displays can engage a group of people, because they are public in nature and they are available for anybody, without needing permission to access the system. This social interaction is a powerful cue for people to pay attention to the display and to communicate with each other. When someone is already interacting with the display or object, there seems to be a higher probability that people passing by would pause and start to play.

1) Walk-Up-and-Use Information Display

The walk-up-and-use information display is designed to encourage a passerby to interact and to respond. Since it is easy to learn, the barrier to start engaging is low, and the public nature of the system results in attracting more people once a single person is attracted. The information on the display provides access to photographs of faculty and the courses they teach. This information is very attractive to the community in this building, and engages passersby to watch the interaction.

2) *The Willful Marionette*

The willful marionette is inherently social because it is located in a museum setting. The 3D human form of the marionette is an attraction because people tend to focus on the human form. The marionette performs a set of gestures even when the Puppet Master is not receiving any gestures from the Kinect. The purpose of these so-called idle gestures is to attract the attention of passersby with the movement of the marionette. Similar to the walk-up-and-use information display, once an individual is attracted to the marionette, others are intrigued and will approach the marionette. *The willful marionette* is able to recognize two participants and encourages social interaction by attending to one person and then shifting attention to a second person. This shift of attention is communicated by rotating the marionette to face a different person.

4.2.4   GESTURE COMMUNICATION

Several advantages are associated with gesture-based interactive systems. According to Kaushik and Jain (2014), gesture-based interactive systems provide a simple, usable, and interesting user interface and satisfy the user's need for more freedom in a human-computer interaction environment. According to Aimaiti and Yan (2011), gesture-based interaction technology provides people with pleasurable new experiences that traditional interaction technology cannot offer and makes the interactions between humans and computers more natural. Instead of learning completely new ways to interact in new scenarios, the users may prefer to adopt the natural channels of communication that they are familiar with in everyday life. These observations have resulted in substantive research on multimodal user interfaces and perceptual user interfaces, in which the user interfaces take advantage of the natural ways that people interact with each other and with the physical world.

1) Walk-Up-and-Use Information Display

Hand gestures are a popular way to interact or control machines, and they have been implemented in many applications. Many other kinds of gestures were explored for this application, but we found that the most common gestures that users would expect are hand gestures. The walk-up-and-use information display system is controlled by free-hand gestures using a Microsoft Kinect–like sensor that recognizes common gestures. To facilitate discoverability, users can learn more about campus information simply by waving at it.

2) *The Willful Marionette*

The design of gesture communication for *the willful marionette* is a challenge because of the high degrees of freedom, and therefore gestures, that can be achieved by string-supported marionettes (Egerstedt et al., 2007; Murphey and Egerstedt, 2008; Murphey and Johnson, 2011). Early designs were trialed and developed to create a design space for communication with the marionette so that engaging movements can be performed. With the design space articulated, specific movement routines can be choreographed and interactive performances achieved by connecting these routines. The human gestures recognized by *the willful marionette* go beyond hand gestures and include full body movements. Similarly, the gestures designed for the marionette response include a broad range of body movement, with very little focus on hand gestures.

4.3   WHAT ARE KEY DESIGN ISSUES FOR GESTURE-BASED INTERACTION?

Gesture-based interaction is becoming more popular, providing interaction designers with great opportunities while also posing great challenges. Some challenges are technical, but more and more the interaction and design challenges are how to ensure that the capabilities of the technology are well matched to the needs and capabilities of the people who use them. There are several perspectives on gesture-based interaction that can inform their design: a better understanding of a cognitive perspective on the roles of gestures (Baber, 2014; Maher et al., 2014; Tversky et al., 2014), the perspective that there should be a common set of gestures (Card, 2014; Jetter, 2014; Karam and Schraefel, 2005), and the perspective of considering the ease of use and effectiveness of gestures for interaction (Ackad et al., 2014; Vanacken and Beznosyk, 2014). In order to elicit a set of popular gestures (Seyed et al., 2012), several researchers have explored the design of gestures that people can easily learn or discover (Cartmill et al., 2012). We identify five issues based on our own experience with gesture-based interaction design:

1. considering how to engage people,

2. designing clear and consistent visual feedback,

3. selecting ergonomic gestures,

4. designing discoverable gestures, and

5. inaccurate gesture recognition.

In this section, we explore these issues with a brief review of the literature, and follow up with how these issues were resolved in the Gesture Commands and Gesture Dialogue systems. Gesture-based interaction is in the early stages of technical and human-centered design research and development. The issues in this section will evolve over time and their resolution will be context dependent.

4.3.1   CONSIDERING HOW TO ENGAGE PEOPLE

There have been many attempts to use mid-air interaction techniques; however, many displays fail to attract the attention of sufficient passersby to exploit the full capabilities of interactions in public spaces (Alt et al., 2012). This section explores how to design interactive user experiences that engage and captivate users. When users pass by a public display, the existence and visualization of movement on the display attracts attention. People can quickly determine whether an interactive display is interesting or not, but it is more difficult to communicate that the display is interactive. As Müller et al. (2010) pointed out, passersby need to notice the display, understand that it is interactive, and be motivated to interact with it. Research is needed to determine how interactive displays can be designed to be more appealing and how designers can leverage interaction onto a screen with a particular focus on public engagement.

Memarovic et al. (2012) described how to enhance public engagement with public interactive displays based on in-depth observations of people interacting with them. When designing public interactive displays, it is important to keep the concept of public engagement in mind, and techniques are needed to encourage user interaction. In the past few decades, public interactive display researchers have emphasized the need to move beyond usability toward understanding how to design systems for more engaging user experiences (O'Brien and Toms, 2008). Creating an engaging experience for the user is important. The user should feel as if he/she is in control of the experience at all times; he/she must constantly feel like he/she is achieving something and be able to see the results of their interaction. An engaging interaction with a mid-air interactive system is not only more enjoyable, but may also be easier to use and more learnable than other types of systems.

1) Walk-Up-and-Use Information Display

The model for gesture-based interaction in the walk-up-and-use information display is a generalized approach to creating interactive public information using a minimal set of gestures for users to explore the information. Information visualization has exploded recently into a large range of techniques for visualizing complex information, with its roots in tools for data exploration and hypothesis formation (Grace et al., 2013). A wide variety of rich data sets (Viégas and Wattenberg, 2007) are visualized in public information displays depending on their purpose. Because information visualization was established in scientific analytical reasoning, the resulting visualizations can be complex and uninteresting to the general public. Users are sometimes overwhelmed by too much information displayed on the screens. This can result in the potential user not approaching the display, or approaching and leaving in frustration because he/she was not able to find information of interest. Since most people are not experts in scientific visualization, the visualization of public information systems should be intuitive to understand, engaging for exploration, and effective in its use of metaphors and themes.

In order to engage users in public space, the walk-up-and-use information display uses the metaphor of a mirror by creating the visualization of the user's shadow showing the movement and actions of the user. This mirror image is designed to attract the user's attention. People observe their shadow images with great curiosity and can use them to experience themselves and their surroundings from new perspectives. Schönböck et al. (2008) stated that making users a part of the display has a strong potential to catch a user's attention as they pass by. Once the passerby's attention has been captured, the walk-up-and-use information display provides instruction to use their hand to interact with the information on the display. The system then engages in a dialogue of user command followed by changing the information display. By providing hints and designing a simple gesture command system, the interaction is easily discovered and learned.

2) *The Willful Marionette*

One of the biggest challenges that distinguish *the willful marionette* from other gesture-based interaction systems is that users in this context are not given instructions. The participants are not expected to do things "in the right way" when communicating with the marionette. The most difficult moment is the cold start when people have no idea what the marionette in front of them can do. Seeing the marionette respond to their presence gives people confidence to initiate or continue gesturing toward the marionette. Users can continue the dialogue after they notice that they have *the willful marionette*'s attention. The interaction was designed so that *the willful marionette* makes the first move and directs its attention to the new user. When rich marionette's actions are performed, it evokes various participants' gestures and guides the participants' focus to the marionette attention. Participants tend to walk around the marionette to find more interesting actions from the marionette. When we added the ability for *the willful marionette* to blink his eyes, we found that eye contact with the marionette is very compelling. It seems that eye contact makes participants feel like they are communicating with an intelligent marionette.

4.3.2   DESIGNING CLEAR AND CONSISTENT VISUAL FEEDBACK

Designing clear and consistent visual feedback is critical in all interaction design contexts; however, it is more critical when the users of the system are casual passersby. In contexts such as desktop or mobile interaction design, the users are exposed to the application repeatedly and have the benefit of familiarity and online support. For gesture interaction design in public displays, this is a significant design issue. Multiple design issues arise: Where is the region in front of the display that is being sensed? What is the range of possible gesture commands? How does the display communicate the possibilities to users? Therefore, gesture-based interaction systems require clear and consistent visible clues about affordances and signifiers (Norman, 2005).

When users try to interact with the system, they can lose interest or their sense of control without appropriate feedback. Without effective feedback, they cannot determine the connections between their actions and the results on the screen. The system should inform users that the system has detected their gestures and show their progress on the screen. Interaction feedback should be designed to alert people to the display's interactivity and mechanisms. How does a person know that the input has been detected and understood by the system? In order for feedback to be effective, it must be immediate, informative, and intelligible. It is necessary to design effective interactive visual feedback that not only provides useful information efficiently, but also engages people to look at the display. The display should be designed to show the information in an attractive and easy-to-understand manner, even from a distance. With interactive visual feedback, a display can convey the concept of gestural commands to users and show users how to use them in a compelling manner.

1) Walk-Up-and-Use Information Display

Showing users where to gesture. In order to interact with the walk-up-and-use information display, users must first be in a place that the gesture-recognition system can sense, otherwise their gestures may not be sensed properly or at all. We give multimodal feedback to help guide users, showing them where they should provide input ("there"). Rather than explicitly guide them, we give feedback telling them how well they can be seen by sensors. This encourages them to explore the input space and form their own understanding of how it works. We do this by estimating how well users can be seen, as a function of the distance between their hand and a sweet spot within sensor view; in this case, this point is the center of the field of view, at a distance where sufficient detail can be sensed. We use shadow color as an indicator, and a distance dialogue is created to provide clear and consistent visual feedback. When objects or the user's hands enter the interaction area, they are displayed in red in contrast with the grey background on the screen. In this manner, users can actively participate in reducing their own errors as they learn to recognize what works and what causes lack of communication with the system. The system provides red and green dot feedback supporting the proper distance between the user and the system. Color is a critical factor for the visibility and readability of the system. The color red seems to be a very natural way to communicate an error state; similarly, the color green intuitively indicates a successful state.

Showing users how to input. Gesture-based interactive systems give users feedback by telling them how well they can be sensed, while also showing them which gesture they need to perform to select it. There are many ways of combining feedback for the "do that" and "there" interactions. The creation of several visual feedbacks helped users learn how to input a selection. Walk-up-and-use information display shows a mirrored shadow of the user, and reacts with optical effects to the gestures of the user, with users being able to more quickly notice interactivity using their own body. To help the user locate his/her hand position relative to the screen, the interacting hand's position is indicated by hand's shadow and color status. Also, the progress bar and 3D bubbles are designed to inform the user that a gesture has been recognized by the system and to show information on their current progress. When one of the bubbles is selected by moving the hand position, it changes from a 2D bubble into a 3D bubble, the progress bar is activated, and once it's finished, a pop-up display is shown. These visual feedbacks provide positive effects such as satisfaction, pleasure, and fun, and enhance the user's understanding of the gestural commands of the system.

2) *The Willful Marionette*

In the design of *the willful marionette*, visual feedback is achieved by the movement of *the willful marionette*. A major design issue was how to give appropriate feedback to participants, since a set of human responses in real life is very different. For example, people are always moving; people respond to a repeated event differently; people may respond by starting a conversation; and people shift their attention to a different object even when nothing happens. To achieve a more life-like marionette, marionette gestures were designed for times when participants are not detected by the Kinect. These idle movements were designed to attract passersby and to achieve a more life-like object. In order to have *the willful marionette* respond differently to identical events, each participant gesture is mapped to a set of possible marionette responses. This one-to-many relationship is used because the goal of the interaction is not to generate an expected response, rather it is to encourage and provoke continued interaction by providing unexpected and novel responses. This is in contrast to the typical interaction design goal of learnable and predictable interaction between user and interface.

4.3.3   SELECTING ERGONOMIC GESTURES

Selecting ergonomic gestures is related to issues in gesture communication such as the technological complexity, learning rate, fatigue, etc. It is important to design feasible ergonomic gestures, since gestural interfaces can be hard to remember and perform for the user. If limited gestures are designed with ergonomic features, this will benefit the users as well as provide a viable solution for having to learn gesture (Nielsen et al., 2003). Fatigue is a well-known issue with gesture-based interaction. Certain ranges of motion can introduce fatigue, and the duration of the interaction, if it requires continuous interaction, can cause fatigue. To avoid fatigue, one common technique for gesture-based selections is to reduce dwell time. When multiple selections are required, dwell time has the potential to exacerbate fatigue effects when a person is required to hold their hand steady. Ergonomics of the surface and the size of hover space are also important factors that affect users' fatigue (Pyryeskin et al., 2012). These challenges have to be considered when determining what gestures people should be expected to be able to use, and whether non-physicality, layers, transitions, and fatigue play a role in those expectations. It is crucial for designers to consider ergonomic features to ensure that a physically stressing gesture is avoided.

1) Walk-Up-and-Use Information Display

The walk-up-and-use information display design addressed the ergonomic affects through user studies of early prototypes. Since there is not a significant literature on how to design to reduce fatigue and other ergonomic considerations, we performed several design and analysis cycles by testing our implementation of gesture designs with user evaluation studies. In our early designs, one issue raised was that the user was required to reach too high to select some items on the screen, and they expressed concern about the reach. In other designs, the dwell time was too long. In our final design, we simplified the gestures and considered the distance between the user and the display so that the hand need not be raised above the shoulder for long periods of time. People's hand gestures are not precise, especially mid-air interaction. A progress bar was designed to show information to the users on their current status or progress. Additionally, the user does not need to hold the hand still during the process, with intent to reduce ergonomic considerations. However, the progress bar function was not noticeable on account of inappropriate size and location. The progress bar was re-designed with conspicuous color, and the size was improved for users to inform immediate feedback. The other issue raised was that the user could not discover the appropriate distance when the system was implemented for the first time. Once the user was located at some point, she/he did not try to move other position even if the location was not proper for interaction. In response to that problem, we designed distance-dialogue feedback to guide users to locate the suitable distance for using the system.

2) *The Willful Marionette*

In *the willful marionette*, the challenge was to design an interactive system as a gesture dialogue between people and a human-like 3D interactive device. We used design methods such as bodystorming and role playing, where members of the design team played either a human participant or a marionette role, and acted out gestural dialogues (See Martin et al., 2012 for descriptions of these design methods). These methods provided a broad range of possible gestures, from which we selected a set of gestures that were easily achieved. Ergonomic issues were not as critical in this design because the participants did not need to perform a specific gesture in order to evoke a response from the marionette. The gestures we selected for the Kinect to recognize included approaching, waving, bending over to look at the marionette, getting too close, and walking away. Other than waving, these gestures are not typical in game playing or as commands in an interactive system. We selected them as movements that the participants perform that would lead to a set of marionette gestures so that interaction was encouraged. They do not have ergonomic considerations because the participant need not perform any of them to evoke a reaction.

4.3.4   DESIGNING DISCOVERABLE GESTURES

It is important to design discoverable gestures in order to avoid interaction blindness. One of challenges encountered by interactive displays is interaction blindness (Grace et al., 2013). People in front of interactive displays are generally unaware of their interactive capabilities, i.e., how they can interact with the displays, and whether gestural interaction is supported. Despite the fact that interactive displays possess important information and/or engage users, it is difficult to make people realize that they can explore them. In addition, users may give up if they do not immediately succeed with their interactions.

Because users expect to see increasingly interactive functionality in displays, gesture design for gesture input methods and real-time visual feedback to the user should be very cautiously considered. The creation of visual feedback and exploration of the interaction in gesture-based systems are challenging because little research to date has focused on characterizing interaction feedback for mid-air display platforms. In our designs, we explored how to engage people near public displays and objects, including the ways they move toward them, congregate around them, and transform from passive viewers into active users. By providing visual interaction feedback, interactive displays and objects can become more effective at alerting users and inducing them to explore their interactive capabilities.

1) Walk-Up-and-Use Information Display

A major design goal for the walk-up-and-use information display is that interaction techniques are easily discovered. In order to determine which gestures are the most easily discovered for our interaction design, we conducted a think-aloud gesture-elicitation study (Morris, 2012) to come up with common intuitive gestures defined by the users. The result of our gesture-elicitation process guided us to focus on gestures made with the hand, and more specifically, gestures that result in a kind of pointing motion. This is the most discoverable gesture for a person that is asked to select or move information on a large display.

2) *The Willful Marionette*

We ran several early user studies of how participants reacted to *the willful marionette* before we implemented the gesture-recognition software. Through several Wizard of Oz sessions, we could observe participants while manually moving the marionette using the Puppet Master application without the gesture-recognition software sending human gesture-recognition data. In our early studies, we noted that generally participants keep a distance between them and the marionette at first. Participants tended to wait to see what the marionette would do. We found that the participants did the gestures like bend over, sit, and approach to be closer to the marionette. Often, the aim of this gesture was to make eye contact with the marionette. Eye contact is one of the most common ways the participant would choose to interact with the marionette. It seems that eye contact makes participants feel they are communicating or interacting with the marionette.

4.3.5   INACCURATE GESTURE RECOGNITION

Much of the research on gesture-based interactions claims that gestures can provide a more natural form of interacting with computers. Gestures are also referred to as a means to enable more natural interactions within public interactive displays since using our hands to manipulate objects is a natural approach to such tasks. But it is precisely the naturalness of the human gesture that challenges gesture-recognition systems. In the literature around gesture-recognition systems, there is a fundamental tension between continuous- and discrete-gesture recognition. As noted above, true human gesture is continuous. Introducing system-required pauses significantly disrupts the natural flow of interactions, but makes implementation easier for the system builders. If the input stream is not artificially segmented in some manner, then designers must deal with segmentation issues themselves. These are not easy issues, as we have no solid guidelines on how segmentation should be done, but they need to be addressed.

Design principles (Norman, 2002; Nielsen, 1994) for interactive systems focus on minimizing users' errors and providing clear feedback indicating causes and solutions for errors. The major cause of error in gesture-based interactive systems is imprecise gestures recognition. If a user performs a gesture and there is no response and no feedback on the screen, users are frustrated. Expecting too much precision leads to mistakes, so interactive systems should allow a wide margin to reduce errors. Interactive systems should provide error notification as response to the users.

1) Walk-Up-and-Use Information Display

The early designs for the walk-up-and-use information display included different hand movements to select, start, stop, and go back. These system responses were part of our gesture-elicitation study. Owing to the difficulty in achieving accuracy in gesture recognition, we reduced the gesture set to a single gesture whose response depended on the context and location on the display. We designed several approaches to providing feedback on the ability to recognize the gesture, and when the gesture was recognized, we provided a clear response.

2) *The Willful Marionette*

The willful marionette does not provide feedback to the participant about gesture recognition. Since a goal of this design was to engage the participant with an intriguing dialogue, we specifically chose not to provide this kind of feedback. In fact, after several months of operating *the willful marionette*, we realized there were inaccuracies in how we implemented the recognition of the "too close" gesture. This did not adversely affect the experience of interacting with the marionette because we specifically did not provide feedback about which gestures could be recognized and which gestures were actually recognized.

CHAPTER 5

Designing for Gesture Interaction

Gesture interaction can take many forms, from simply using a hand to target something on the screen to specific continuous movement using the whole body. Until recently, mid-air gestures have not been part of interaction design. Implementing gestures as part of the interaction design requires a careful consideration of the types of gestures that are meaningful in the system. Furthermore, it is important for the user to understand which gestures can be recognized by the interactive system. Defining a set of gestures for interactive systems should reduce confusion on the part of the user. If the gesture is too circumscribed, unique, or complex, it will be difficult for the user to perform. If the gesture is too generic or simple, it will be easier for the user to perform, but might conflict with other gestures (Seyed et al., 2012). This section describes how we designed the walk-up-and-use information display and *the willful marionette* by considering the context of use, the design goals, the technology selection, design methods specific to gesture-based interaction, and the interaction model.

5.1   DESIGNING THE WALK-UP-AND-USE INFORMATION DISPLAY

5.1.1   CONTEXT OF USE

With the advent of affordable large display screens, university buildings are hosting large displays within the hallways and vestibules to serve as electronic bulletin boards running a slide show of information. Numerous large display systems have been implemented to explore and share information in a university setting, but they're not interactive; they do not provide any additional functionality that could not already be provided by a website. Walk-up-and-use information display is an interactive system that provides the capability of free-hand gestures, enabling a more engaging and natural form of interaction. This system is intended to be a framework for students to use to explore the various classes, instructors, research, and student organizations within the context of a college/department at the University of North Carolina at Charlotte. For their purposes, the display was more along the lines of an informational system that provided users with the ability to see how classes interconnected through prerequisite courses and disciplines. Moreover, the application can be scaled to cover multiple departments or colleges.

5.1.2   DESIGN GOALS

The design goals for the walk-up-and-use information display are to design a discoverable interaction system for mid-air gestures, to design an engaging and enjoyable experience on a public display, and to enhance gesture recognition in a university setting.

Discoverable Interaction System. A walk-up-and-use information display is intended to enable users to discover innovative new ways of navigating through the information displayed, making our system more accessible and easy to use. In order to achieve this design goal, a clear relationship between the gesture completed and the response of the application should be designed for users to learn how to use the application in an appropriate time frame.

Engaging Interaction. In order for an application to be truly effective, users must be enticed to interact with the system as they pass by. This is done by offering appropriate visual feedback that the system is interactive, and can be communicated with. As well as enticing the user to begin initial use of the application, the system is designed to keep them engaged in order for the useful transmission of information to occur. Some form of mirrored display was selected for this task, showing users that the device can see them, and initiating gesture interaction.

Gesture Recognition. A walk-up-and-use information display must improve upon the ability to recognize the intent of the user. This goal is achieved through the design of new gesture interactions such as an average point tracking system that are both clearer for the user and more legible for the Kinect.

5.1.3   TECHNOLOGY SELECTION

1) Application

Figure 5.1 is an illustration of the walk-up-and-use information display application showing course information for the Software and Information Systems (SIS) department for the 2015 spring semester. Five clusters of SIS courses, namely, HCI, Health Informatics, Intelligent Systems, Security, and Software Systems, are distinguished with different colors. Course information is presented to users in the form of the course number, course name, instructor, and a brief description of the course. When the system is activated by the user, the user is presented with a screen displaying the course information clustered by department. Users can use their hands to interact with the system. Hand movement plays the role of a cursor, allowing the user to delve into the cluster and explore the information presented in greater detail. When one of the clusters is selected, detailed pop-up information is also displayed on the screen. The user can employ a similar method to gain more detailed information about specific types of related information.

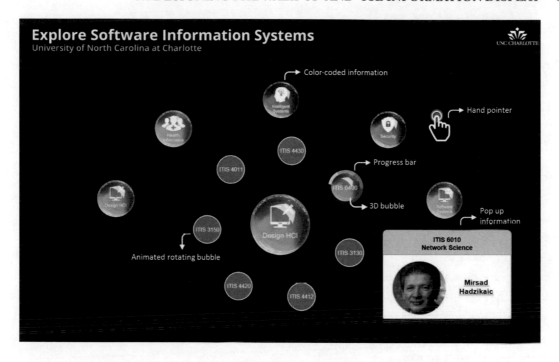

Figure 5.1: Walk-up-and-use information display application.

2) Technology

The software system that implements the gesture interaction is responsible for recognizing the users' gestures and mapping them onto the appropriate corresponding actions. The mirror concept was used to contribute to enticing interaction on public displays, performing bodily gestures to control a mirror-image representation of self on a display. In order to express mirror image, gesture recognition is influenced by the capabilities of the Microsoft Kinect device used for sensing the user's intent. Generally, the Microsoft Kinect software development kit (SDK) has been used to capture users' skeleton-stream data from a Kinect camera to map each gesture to its corresponding action. Instead of the skeleton tracking, which is a general way of capturing motion, an average point-tracking system is employed; this was originally implemented in Daniel Shiffman's OpenKinect processing libraries (http://shiffman.net/2011/01/13/new-kinect-example-average-point-tracking/), which offer the users a mirrored display that aids them in learning how the system works. This means that the Kinect establishes a stable threshold an appropriate distance from the screen, and any points found by the Infrared (IR) sensor within that threshold are averaged to create a cursor. Therefore, the user can stand outside the threshold and reach in with one hand to manipulate this cursor. This system is still susceptible to errors, but we found that offering the users a mirrored display aided them in learning how the system works. Many researchers have continued the efforts in advanced point-cloud processing, making it more powerful, and offering features such as displaying normally, drawing shapes, and multiple viewports.

5.1.4   DESIGN METHODS

1) Design Concept: Mirror

The idea of the mirror concept is to create the illusion of a shadow that is controlled by a given user by mimicking the motions and actions of the user. Many people enjoy interactive displays for public spaces on the basis of the mirrored shadow image of the user because the design principle is intuitive and encourages playful interactions with whole-body gestures. These systems are considered to possess potentially engaging interaction components for users. This shadow image serves to attract the user's attention. For example, when users look at the display and notice their own projected shadows, they can initiate subtle interactions, and if they are convinced that the display is reacting to them, their curiosity may be raised. They can start to directly interact and play with the system by walking back and forth and playing with their shadow images. A mirrored display helps users to learn how the system works.

2) Gesture Design

In order to determine which gestures are the most easily discovered for interaction design, a think-aloud gesture-elicitation study (Morris, 2012) was conducted to come up with common intuitive gestures defined by the users. End users were individually shown the desired effect of an action (called a referent) and were asked to perform the gesture that would bring about that effect. The results from all participants were analyzed to create a final gesture set using metrics such as agreement, max-consensus, or consensus-distinct ratio (Wobbrock et al., 2005, 2009).

- Referent 1: selecting a particular cluster from the base screen.

- Referent 2: expanding a node within the selected cluster.

- Referent 3: returning to the originally selected cluster from an expanded node.

- Referent 4: returning to the base screen from an expanded cluster.

- Referent 5: selecting another cluster without returning to the base screen.

These referents cover the system's entire set of features. The participants were asked to come up with at least four gestures per referent that he or she would use to perform the required actions.

The think-aloud method (Boren and Ramey, 2000) is used, which involves asking participants to verbalize their thoughts while performing their tasks. The gathered verbalizations can complement the observation, while making conclusions. The participants were video recorded while performing the gestures. These videos were analyzed using the protocol analysis technique, and the participant gestures were coded into a total of nine distinct categories:

- Pointing and Clicking

- Swiping and Wiping

- Dragging

- Lassoing

- Zooming

- Rotating

- Hovering

- Full-Body Movement (not limited to arms)

- Pushing and Pulling

The following shows the results of the gesture-elicitation study. The swipe, zoom, and point gestures were the most common among participants. During the system implementation, we started off by coding the swipe, zoom, and point gesture recognition for each referent. Our intent was that the system would recognize the different gestures and their corresponding referents. However, there were recognition issues with the swipe and zoom gestures because of the display size and information layout on the screen. Therefore, the point gesture was finalized as the most intuitive gesture.

- Referent 1: selecting a particular cluster from the base screen.

  For Referent 1, the most common gestures were point/click, zoom, and swipe/wipe. The zoom gesture was expected to occur when the user goes deeper into the application to get more information and then reverses to zoom out. Point/click did occur at the same frequency as zoom and was also a quite natural gesture for the users to assume.

- Referent 2: expanding a node within the selected cluster.

  For referent 2, the most common gesture was point/click followed closely by zoom and swipe/wipe. This was consistent with the previous referent's results, which we took to be a positive thing because the referents are closely aligned (opening a cluster, opening a node).

- Referent 3: returning to the originally selected cluster from an expanded node.

    For referent 3, the most common gestures were point/click, swipe/wipe, zoom, and full-body movements. The top gestures from the previous referents were consistent here with the addition of the body-movement gesture. It's interesting that there wasn't a clear most-common gesture for this referent, perhaps because the users could not find a very clear way to navigate back in the system.

- Referent 4: returning to the base screen from an expanded cluster.

    For referent 4, the most common gestures were consistent with referent 3, with a slight edge up in zoom and point/click. Because this is the same type of referent as referent 3 (close node, close cluster), the research team expected the gestures selected to be similar.

- Referent 5: selecting another cluster without returning to the base screen.

    For referent 5, the most common gesture was swipe/wipe followed by point/click. This is the only referent for which swipe/wipe was the solitary top gesture; however, the secondary gesture was common throughout all referents.

5.1.5   INTERACTION MODEL

The gesture interaction model will be described based on the interaction phase. The system adapts to the user in four interaction phases. If there is no user nearby, the display remains in ambient mode to enable users to get a general overview of the information at a quick glance. When users first look at the display, they might move their arms to get a reaction from the display. Later, they might change their location to the center of the displays to interact more with the system. If users approach the display, they can interact with it using gestures in subtle interactions. If users are interested in interacting further with the system, they can actively interact with it by producing a variety of gestures.

1) Passing by and Viewing

Anyone who happens to be present in the specified vicinity of a gesture-based interactive system can be called a passerby. The specific area depends on the particular type of interactive system, and in principle, should include anyone who can see the system. This area should generally be restricted to only those people who are sufficiently close to the system that they can observe it. As soon as a passerby shows any observable reaction to the system, such as looking at it, smiling, or turning his/her head, he/she is considered a viewer, and the system is activated.

This interface presents a conversational hook to the users, providing them with a simple message to convey the system's interactivity. The interface presents a mirror image to the user that shows the user's own silhouette on the screen.

Figure 5.2: Walk-up-and-use information display: Idle Mode.

2) Subtle Interaction

As soon as the viewer shows any signs of movement, it should elicit some reaction from the system. This might happen when a viewer briefly pauses in front of the system. Subtle interaction occurs several meters away from the system, where the user does not occupy any part of the system. This allows for the simultaneous interaction of others.

When a user is detected, the interface tries to captivate him/her with a greeting message and can also maintain the user's attention by displaying animated rotating bubbles and shadow images. When objects or the user's hands enter the interaction area, they are displayed as red in contrast to the screen's grey background. In this manner, users can actively participate in reducing their own errors as they begin to recognize what works and what causes problems for the system.

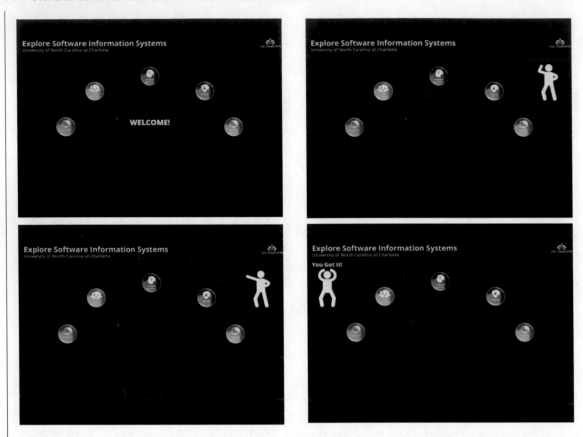

Figure 5.3: Walk-up-and-use information display: subtle interaction mode.

3) Direct Interaction

After a few initial subtle interactions, users typically try to position themselves at the center of the system. This coincides with the user entering a relatively small area within about 1 m of the system. Once the user is located within the interaction zone, he/she actively engages the display for a period of time.

When the user is actively interacting with the system, it presents a distance dialogue that helps users to find the appropriate distance for using the system. The system responds with visual feedback based on the user's distance from the system. If the user is too close, the system will present an error message such as "You are too close," and if the user is too far away, the system will present a message such as "Come closer." This distance dialogue between the user and the system provides positive effects such as satisfaction, pleasure, and fun, and enhances the user's understanding of the system.

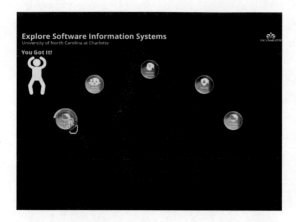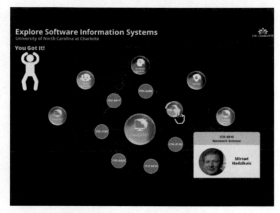

Figure 5.4: Walk-up-and-use information display: direct interaction mode.

4) Leaving

In this phase, users are not located within the interaction area. If the user is located outside the interaction range of the system, the system returns to the ambient display phase. This phase produces a central context that anchors all subsequent interaction and gives the user an overview of what types of information or interactive functions the system offers. When users are not in the interaction area, the system reverts to idle mode and displays conversational dialogue to entice other users to interact with it.

5.1.6   DESIGN HEURISTICS

Heuristic evaluation is a UI evaluation method proposed by Nielsen and Molich (1990). The goal of heuristic evaluation is to find usability problems in an existing UI design, so they can be fixed. Heuristic evaluation is performed by usability professionals who evaluate a UI design against a set of accepted usability principles called evaluation heuristics. The severity and location of each problem is noted, and evaluators provide their opinions on how to improve the UI. Nielsen and Molich argued that heuristic evaluation is an inexpensive and effective alternative to formal empirical user testing.

Nielsen (1994) classified heuristics that explained the majority of usability problems;

- visibility of system status;

- match between system and the real world;

- user control and freedom;

- consistency and standards;

- error prevention;

- recognition rather than recall;

- flexibility and efficiency of use;

- aesthetic and minimalist design;

- help users recognize, diagnose and recover from errors; and

- help and documentation.

Nielsen developed his heuristics primarily for evaluation of desktop applications. Since Nielsen's heuristics are regarded as suitable for generic usability evaluation, they can be adapted for mid-air interactive displays; however, no evaluation heuristics have been specialized for mid-air interactive displays. Existing heuristics have been used as a starting point to develop interactive display heuristics. The goal in this section is to develop a new set of heuristics that can be used by interactive display designers to evaluate both early mockups and functional prototypes. A new set of heuristics is introduced that can be used to carry out usability inspections of mid-air interactive displays. The heuristics are developed to help identify usability problems in both early and functional interface prototypes.

A new set of heuristics is considered that are applicable to the mid-air interactive system. First, the heuristics can serve as a set of design principles that can be used during the formative stages of interaction design and development. Second, they can be used to carry out usability inspections where evaluators use them to critique the design. The heuristics concerning the special properties of mid-air interactive displays have been developed through literature review and in collaboration with two HCI experts. Nielsen's title was used but redefined as much as possible keep his definition because it will be easy to explain to people who know this already. Two additional heuristics, "provocative interaction" and "muscle fatigue," were added, which have significant differences from the original definition.

Visibility of System Status. The interactive public display should provide feedback on user's key actions in a clear manner and within a reasonable time. Users should be able to clearly identify their interaction location within the application, and their available options. In order to provide a clear understanding of system usage and information navigation, showing system status with visual feedback is necessary for effective interaction design. The interactive display should provide navigational feedback such as showing a user's current and initial states, where they have been, and what options they have for where to go.

Match between the System and the Real World. The interactive public display should be designed with familiar user interface metaphors and analogies to help users understand the system. Interactive applications should use specific conventions of the real world and should show the information in an easy-to-discover order. The sequence of activities and gestures for using a mid-air interactive system should follow a user's mental processes. Metaphors should be easy to understand, with natural, intuitive gestures; there should be an intuitive mapping between controls and their functions.

User Control and Freedom. Nielsen's original definition of user control and freedom is: "Users often choose system functions by mistake and will need a clearly marked 'emergency exit' to leave the unwanted state without having to go through an extended dialogue. Support undo and redo" (Nielsen, 1994, p. 30) Offering this function is not relevant to interactive public displays, but the concepts of user control and freedom are still important. If the user feels that the system is difficult to use, the result can be disinterest during usage of the system. Therefore, the user needs to feel not only in control of his or her own gestures and movements, but also in control of the manner in which they explore the system. This heuristic is also related to navigation. Users should easily move through the system and information of interest.

Consistency and Standards. The interactive public display should be designed to present similar elements in similar ways. Consistency with real-world conventions and affordances of the visual references is important. Gestures should be consistent throughout the different states of the system. Gestural interfaces are more powerful but less discoverable than traditional interaction such as clickable interfaces. Mid-air gestures can feel removed from the display when compared with traditional clickable touch or mouse interaction, so clear affordances and consistent interaction are critical for this kind of interaction to work well.

Error Prevention. Interactive interface design should provide appropriate interaction in order to prevent users' errors and provide clear feedback indicating causes and solutions for errors. The major cause of error in mid-air gesture interactive public displays is imprecise gestures recognition. If the system recognizes and responds to a gesture but no visual feedback is provided, users will be frustrated. Expecting too much precision in performing the gesture leads to mistakes, so to reduce errors, an interactive system should allow a wide margin for gesture recognition. The interactive system should provide error notification in response to the users' errors in performing the gesture.

Recognition rather than Recall. The relationship between controls and user's gestures should be obvious. Input formats and units of values should be indicated to minimize the user's memory load. Gestures should be designed to be understandable and intuitive so that a user can easily learn how to use the system without difficulties or memorizing all gestures.

Flexibility and Efficiency of Use. The interactive public display should offer appropriate guide to novice users. Experienced users should get appropriate mechanism to utilize applications according to their needs, skills, and personal preferences.

Aesthetic and Minimalist Design. The system should not overload users with irrelevant and unnecessary information. The interactive public display should show concise information. The data structure should be designed so that it is easy to learn. Related pieces of information should be clustered together and the amount of information should be minimized to easily explore information with gestures interaction.

Help. Nielsen's original definition of help and documentation for desktop application was considered necessary: designers should provide help and documentation. Providing this traditional form of documentation for the interactive public display does not make sense since the use of the system is voluntary and optional. The meaning of help is very different in the interactive public display because help should be part of the user experience, not a separate document.

Provocative Interaction. The interactive public display should engage users to maintain their attention and interest, evoke their curiosity, and be emotionally engaging. The interaction design should display visual effects and animations that can be manipulated by a user with movement of a hand or body for a fun and novel experience. Provocative interaction is a new term for mid-air interaction heuristics. When Nielsen developed a set of heuristics for desktop application, there was no need to be provocative or engaging. The words engaging, fun, and interesting don't appear in his heuristics at all. The original heuristics were developed for desktop applications that people use for work or other productivity purposes, whereas the interactive public display should be considered engaging in a public space.

Muscle Fatigue. Nielsen's heuristics did not include ergonomic considerations because they were thought of as separate from the interactive application and were more associated with the human factors design of the screen, keyboard, and mouse. The design of the interactive public display changes the ergonomics. In this new context of use, the designer should avoid repetitive or prolonged gestures that cause fatigue. This fatigue will cause users to walk away or decrease the precision of the intended gestures and affect performance.

5.2   DESIGNING *THE WILLFUL MARIONETTE*

5.2.1   CONTEXT OF USE

The willful marionette is a collaborative interaction design project between two artists, Lilla LoCurto and Bill Outcault, with the Interaction Design Lab at the University of North Carolina at Charlotte. The project is driven by the artists, whose previous work focuses on the human body as a 3D form, and its representation in space. The artists wanted to create a marionette that would be fully automatic and interact with people via gestures only. The context of use is a public location such as an art museum, and the interaction is voluntary. The artists were interested in provoking an emotional response and raising awareness of the frailty of the human body. *The willfull marionette* is a 3D printed scan of the full body of one of the artists, with joints and strings so that it can move in a way that is similar to marionette artform and performance. Rather than being controlled by a puppeteer, the marionette is controlled by software we call the Puppet Master (Mahzoon et al., 2016).

Artists nowadays are working with engineers and researchers to explore the possibility of integrating robotics into the marionette performance, for example Yamane et al. (2004). In previous work on developing a robotic marionette, researchers explored the possibility of infusing robotic systems into the traditional art form of Marionette Theater (Chen et al., 2005) to evoke and stimulate public interest (Robert et al., 2011; Sidner et al., 2005; Speed et al., 2014). The automated marionctte suggests an interactive relationship between art object and audience member. Typically, the audience member is a passive viewer who watches the marionette as the puppeteer performs in a theatrical setting. With an interactive marionettc, the audience becomes active participants in the art, and without the context of a theatrical performance to capture the viewers' attention, the puppet must act as provocateur to engage the viewer. Once engaged, the participants continue to interact with *the willful marionette* and to evoke the movements and reactions of the puppet. Interaction dcsign in this context is about the interaction between participants (not users) and the 3D marionette (not a computer screen). While creating an interaction between the art installation and the audience/participants is not a new kind of artistic expression, *the willful marionette* focuses on the movement of the human body (both person and machine) and on creating a dialogue of gestures that provoke movement and evoke emotional response.

5.2.2   DESIGN GOALS

Traditionally, the marionette is manipulated by a puppeteer. With no puppeteer, the marionette is merely an inanimate object. Our primary goal in this project is to design the interaction so that the marionette can be fully automatic and interact with people in an artistic way. The artists' intention for *the willful marionette* is to evoke a gesture dialogue between people and a human-like 3D interactive device that provokes an emotional response.

Computational creativity. The synthesis of a traditional art form, the marionette, with a modality of human-machine interaction limited to gesture interaction, is a kind of computational creativity: the evocation of a creative dialogue of gestures between humans and human-like machines. To achieve this design goal, *the willful marionette* is designed to provoke a unique and ongoing dialogue between people and a 3D replica of a human body, where the dialogue comprises only full-body movements and gestures.

Gesture sets for interaction. In contrast to studies on the mechanics and technologies for creating robotic marionettes, *the willful marionette* is designed with a focus on the user experience, an interaction model for gesture-based dialogue, and gestures sets for a dialogue that provokes an emotional response. In this context, the artifacts being designed include: (1) the human gestures that *the willful marionette* is able to recognize and (2) the marionettes gestures that provoke and respond to the participants.

Engagement in a public place. *The willful marionette* is designed to encourage people to engage in a gesture-based dialogue in a public setting. To engage viewers in a public place, the marionette performs idle actions that try to attract attention. The marionette is designed as the prime mover or initiator of interaction.

5.2.3   TECHNOLOGY SELECTION

1) Gesture Recognition and Execution

The software system that implements the marionette gesture interaction has three components: participant gesture detection, marionette gesture selection, and marionette gesture execution. The participant gesture-detection component uses the Microsoft Kinect and Kinect SDK library to detect and send human gestures to the marionette gesture-selection program. The selection component selects the most relevant marionette gesture to execute, and sends the related command to the gesture-execution component. The gesture-execution component activates servo motors via an Arduino board to raise and lower specific joints via strings.

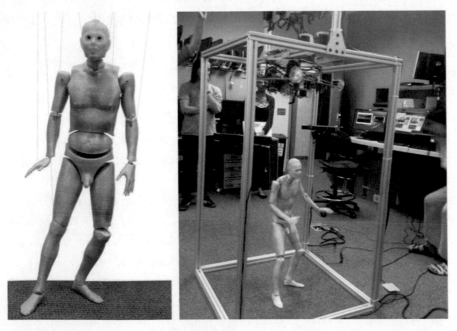

Figure 5.5: *The willful marionette.*

2) Construction

The construction of the marionette started with a 3D scan of a human body that was used to construct a 3D printed marionette. *The willful marionette*, standing about 3 feet tall as shown in Figure 5.5, is a replica of a naked adult male body using 3D scanning and printing techniques. To create the marionette, the whole body was segmented into 17 parts. Segments are connected with hinge joints and socket joints according to the corresponding joints on human body. Thirteen of the joints are connected to strings to enable movement. The movement of the strings is controlled by motors connected to a frame above *the willful marionette*, enabling joints to move up and down. In addition, inside *the willful marionette's* head there is a standby motor that controls his eyelids. Two Microsoft Kinects are attached to the frame to capture the movement of people around *the willful marionette*. *The willful marionette* moves as a response to the movement of people around him. The marionette has a computational core that creates a sequence of gestures that provoke and respond to the gestures of the people nearby. Through the use of sensor technology and the autonomous motorized control of the marionette, the project explores the tendency of humans to ascribe emotional characteristics to a machine with a human form.

5.2.4   DESIGN METHODS

1) User-Experience Research

Various design methods, such as bodystorming, role-playing, personas, and image boards, were used in the early stages of the project to explore and develop ideas for a user experience that is limited to gesture interaction. These methods provided the design team with the opportunity to explore the range of gestures performed as an interaction dialogue in the context of the software and technologies to be used in the development phase. In bodystorming and role-playing, members of the design team played either a human participant or a marionette role in acting out how the two might interact using only gestures. Figure 5.6 illustrates body movements of people and the marionette as a design space for human gesture recognition and marionette gesture movement.

On the basis of the initial prototypes and the results of bodystorming, a set of preliminary gestures were designed and implemented for the marionette. Marionette gestures were created by moving joints connected to stepper motors via strings. Each gesture was defined by specifying each motor's movement in time. This definition allowed the design team to write and store gestures in a file and label them for future use, i.e. when the system selects a marionette gesture to be executed in response to a human gesture. In the next phase of the design, a think-aloud gesture-elicitation study was conducted to explore the different human gestures in the context of marionette gesture responses.

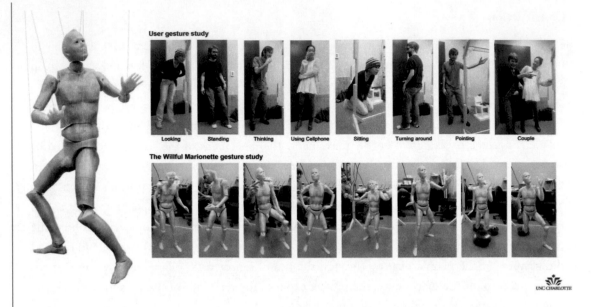

Figure 5.6: Bodystorming: exploring interactions between humans and the marionette.

2) Gesture-Elicitation Study

The design process included abstracting a participant's behavior into meaningful gestures and designing and implementing marionette actions. To recognize complex and sophisticated human actions as discrete gestures, a gesture-elicitation study was performed for both human gesture and marionette gesture classifications. The Wizard of Oz technique was used to operate the marionette in the presence of participants. A few scenarios were planned for the gesture-elicitation study. To attract the attention of the participant, the marionette was controlled to raise his head and look directly at the participant's face. When a participant approached the marionette, the marionette was controlled to raise his hands and crouch as if to say "don't come closer." The marionette performed tracking actions during which the marionette would rotate to follow the movement of the participant. The marionette expressed idling actions through subtle movements of the strings, such as "breathe" and "shake his head," which were intended to represent human-like behaviors. In this study, a human operator decided which marionette gesture to execute based on participants' gestures. The initial user study included 12 participants. Each participant was asked to interact with the marionette spontaneously without specifying a specific task. Participants were asked to think aloud while interacting with the marionette. After each session, an interview was conducted to collect additional insights about participants' gesture behavior. Video recording was used to capture each performed gesture along with notes taken by the design team. The human gestures selected to be included in the gesture-recognition component were based on an analysis of the video and interview data that identified the most commonly used gestures during the Wizard of Oz study.

Table 5.1: Results of gesture-elicitation study		
Body Portion	**Gestures**	**# of times**
Head	Tilt head (1), head down (1)	2
Body	Sit(3), bend over(7), back off(2), turn around(2)	14
Arm/Hand	Fold hands (6), fold arms (2), raise hand (22), open arms (6), hands on waist (9), hands on face (5), shake hand (3), wave hand (5), touch (1)	59
Leg	Cross leg (3), approach (all), walk away (all), go to the left side (8), go to the right side (3), go to the back (6)	44
	Total	119

As a result of the gesture-elicitation study, a list of gestures was compiled as shown in Table 5.1. The gestures are grouped according to the portion of the body that moves to enact the gesture: the head, whole-body movement, the arms and hands, and the legs. The list of gestures is shown with an indication of how many times that gesture was observed across all 12 participants. In total, 21 different gestures were identified; and a total of 119 of these gestures were performed. The following principles were applied to reduce the set of gestures performed in the gesture-elicitation study to the set that would be recognized by *the willful marionette*.

- Gestures were eliminated that are not clearly directed at the marionette. For example, gestures like "turn around," "raise hand," and "hand on face."

- Some gestures are not a response to the marionette's behavior. For example, gestures like "cross leg," "hands on waist," and "tilt head" were eliminated.

- Some gestures are too hard to detect correctly with the Kinect, such as "fold arms" and "fold hands."

One of the biggest challenges that distinguishes *the willful marionette* from other gesture-based interaction systems is that users in this context are not given instructions. The participants are not expected to do things "in the right way" when communicating with *the willful marionette*. The most difficult moment is the cold start when people have no idea what the marionette in front of them can do. Seeing the marionette respond to their presence gives people confidence to initiate or continue gesturing toward the marionette. Participants are more willing to continue the dialogue after they notice that they got the marionette's attention. The interaction is designed so that the marionette makes the first move and directs its attention to the new participant. That is the reason for detecting a participant approaching the marionette. Similarly, walking away is also a meaningful gesture showing that the participant has lost interest in the marionette.

The final participant gestures to be recognized are: approaching, waving, bending over, getting too close, walking away. In addition to identifying common gestures in response to the movements of the marionette, the gesture-elicitation study and the interviews revealed that lifting the marionette's head to make eye contact, turning the marionette's body to follow the person (tracking), and raising hands were the most impressive ones among the initial marionette gestures.

5.2.5   INTERACTION MODEL

Our interaction model has two sets of gestures: the human gestures that trigger a response from the marionette and the marionette gestures. The interaction model for *the willful marionette* describes the mapping from a recognized human gesture to a marionette gesture. The set of human gestures in the interaction model are:

- approach;

- too close;

- bend over;

- wave; and

- walk away.

The marionette gestures were designed to communicate an emotional state. The marionette gestures were grouped into the following emotional responses:

Complex gestures. A subset of the marionette gestures involves large body movements that are intended to convey that the marionette is experiencing a strong emotional response. These gestures are implemented as a quickly executed series of movements across many degrees of freedom. Examples of the marionette's complex gestures include surprise and scared.

Subtle gestures. Other, smaller gestures are intended to encourage continued interaction with the marionette. For instance, simply lifting the head of the marionette gives an impression of eye contact and, in our experiments, engaged participants and made them more likely to continue interacting. Similarly, a series of movements that convey a quizzical look from the marionette while participants wave at him can be intriguing and encourages continued interaction.

Attentive gestures. These gestures are a direct response to participants' movement. For example, the marionette turns so that it tracks a participant, or turns its head such that it faces them. As another example, when participants walk away from the marionette, the marionette might shake its head as an attentive gesture to get their attention back.

Living gestures. These gestures are designed to convey the impression that the marionette is alive, and involve movement that is not a direct response to perceived participant action. For example, the marionette possesses a motor behind its eyes that can execute a blinking gesture, which is performed at random times. Another example of this type of gesture is a "breathing" gesture, which moves the back of the marionette up and down very slowly such that it looks like it is breathing. These gestures prevent the marionette from being completely still.

Restorative gestures. After performing some gestures, the marionette might not be in a natural pose, or may have lost track of its exact pose owing to technical limitations. To accommodate this lack of information, a restorative gesture was designed to adjust the marionette's position back to its initial position. One such gesture slightly lifts marionette up off the ground and returns it to its default position.

The design of appropriate marionette response gestures to participant gestures was based on the consideration of a number of emotional states that may cause the participant to perform a particular gesture. Rather than attempt to interpret an emotional stance for each participant gesture, a set of marionette responses was designed for assumed emotional stances, such as curious, shy, or skeptical. The design team then constructed a probability that participants would be in each emotional state, and developed the interaction model by selecting a weighted random gesture from a set of possible gestures associated with each recognized human gesture. This allowed the marionette to respond to the most likely emotional state of the participant (a person bent over is typically interested in the marionette), without the ability to detect or infer meaning. Table 5.2 shows the mapping from each human gesture to the set of marionette gestures that were placed in the emotional-state categories.

Table 5.2: The mapping from human gesture to marionette gesture in *the willful marionette*	
Human Gestures	**Marionette Gestures**
Approach	scared, shirk, surprised
Wave	stand straight, quizzical look
Bend over	surprised, shocked, shirk
Walk away	surprised, shy, shake head
Too close	shy, shake head, stand straight, look up fast, walk backward

The marionette gesture-selection component is also responsible for deciding which participant is important. Participant importance is decided by their continued engagement (measured by amount of body movement) and the order that people approach the marionette. These important participants are then tracked and the marionette rotates to follow their position. From the gesture-elicitation study and participant interviews, it was determined that eye contact was the most important feature to participants, and resulted in the highest level of engagement. If a person was to the left or right of the marionette and no one was present in front, the marionette would rotate to face the new person, and gestural interaction would continue. The absence of human movement would trigger an idle state, during which the marionette would perform subtle gestures in an attempt to engage nearby people.

The interaction model can be further understood as comprising a set of phases: "passing by and viewing," "subtle interaction," "direct interaction," and "leaving."

Passing by and viewing: When a user approaches the marionette, the marionette presents living gestures. Some gestures were designed to move the marionette in a way that looks like it is alive. For instance, there is a motor for the eyes of the marionette that performs an eye blinking gesture with randomized timing. Another example of this type of gesture is a gesture that can be called breathing. This gesture moves the back of the marionette up and down very slowly such that it looks like it is breathing.

Subtle interaction: When participant goes out of the range of the sensors, the marionette performs subtle gestures. These are smaller gestures intended to encourage people to continue interacting with the marionette. For example, simply lifting the head of the marionette gives an impression of eye contact, and the participants found this particularly engaging. This sequence is illustrated in Figure 5.7.

Figure 5.7: Looking down and up to create a sense of making eye contact.

Direct interaction: In this interaction phase, the participant is waving, bending over, and getting too close to the marionette. The marionette performs a set of complex gestures and attentive gestures. Complex gestures are large body movements that are intended to convey a strong emotional response from the marionette. More technically, these gestures are implemented as a quickly executed series of movements that cause the marionette to move to a new totally different position. Figure 5.8 (a, b) shows examples of this kind of gesture. In Figure 5.8 (a), the marionette is raising both hands and crouching down and away from the person. In Figure 5.8 (b) the marionette is lifting one leg to turn in another direction. Attentive gestures are created to have a direct response to participants' movement. For example, the marionette turns so that it tracks the people nearby, or the marionette turns its head such that it faces the people nearby.

Figure 5.8: (a): Complex gesture with hands up, head down and knees bent. (b): Complex gesture with raised knee while rotating the entire body to the left.

Leaving: After performing some gestures, the marionette might not be in a natural pose because of a lack of feedback on the location of all joints. To accommodate this lack of information, another kind of gesture was designed to adjust the marionette's position back to its initial, contemplative position. The implementation of this gesture is to lift the marionette up from the ground and put it back where it was. This gesture causes the marionette to return to its default position.

5.2.6   DESIGN GUIDELINES

The willful marionette represents a contemporary interpretation of the marionette as a form of performance. By replacing the puppeteer and puppet with an automated marionette, the act of performance and interaction becomes more physically engaging even as it removes the human-to-human interaction that would occur if a puppeteer were present. By exposing the way the marionette is controlled, the marionette achieves abstract human characteristics that are unnerving and fascinating at the same time. By leveraging technology as a reinterpretation of a traditional art form, the typical art experience of static viewership is altered, allowing the viewers and art to interact in unexpected ways.

The gesture-interaction design principles developed through this design process are:

- **Recognize simple body movements to trigger the marionette response.** This allows the gesture-recognition software to be efficient and elegant. The categories of gestures recognized relevant to this contest are: waving, bending over, approaching, walking away, and getting too close to the marionette. These categories were constructed to recognize motion that will initiate or continue a dialogue.

- **Randomly select the marionette response from a set of possible responses.** This gives the marionette an air of intrigue. Many participants continued interacting to see if they could find a pattern in the responses, and would often assume that the marionette was thinking about its response.

- **Design marionette movements to evoke a response from the human participants.** A set of gesture categories were defined to give the marionette a kind of personality by creating gestures that could be interpreted as a human-like emotional response. *The willful marionette* gesture categories constructed for this context were: complex, subtle, attentive, living, and contemplative.

To improve responsiveness of the system, motor movements and the timing of each marionette gesture were recorded in a separate file. After a gesture has been selected, the system calls for the execution of the related file. The gestures of the marionette were divided into two categories on the basis of its responsiveness. The first category is a set of "regular" gestures that are selected in response to participants' gestures, and the second one is a set of "idle" movements that are selected when no one interacts with the marionette for a defined amount of time. Idle movements are actions that are short in terms of execution time, and are subtle movements designed to engage people to interact. This categorization caused the marionette to continually execute gestures, and, in a way, brings it to life.

There are many ways to improve on *the willful marionette*. One is to reconsider the random selection of marionette responses, and replace randomness with machine learning or artificial intelligence (AI) models. For example, a clustering algorithm could create profiles of specific participants, and the marionette response could be guided by the gestures already generated in response to a specific person. Alternatively, the curious agent model that is proposed in (Saunders and Gero, 2004) could be adapted to imbue curiosity into *the willful marionette*. This computational model of curiosity uses a novelty detection algorithm to evaluate "interestingness." In *the willful marionette*, this model of curiosity could look for novel patterns of human participant gestures and respond to those that are interesting.

CHAPTER 6

Looking to the Future: Research Challenges

In this book we present the concepts and significance of embodied interaction design, specifically for tangible and gesture-based interaction. Embodied interaction is very different from the way that we traditionally communicate with machines because the user can use their body in ways in which they are used to using them in the natural physical world to interact with digital systems. Creating embodied interactive systems is challenging for a number of reasons, including technical and research. In this chapter, we present our understanding of the challenges in embodied interaction design from two different perspectives: design challenges and research challenges.

6.1 DESIGN CHALLENGES FOR EMBODIED INTERACTION

6.1.1 UNDERSTANDING EMBODIED ACTIONS AS USER INPUT

One challenge to embodied interaction is that it is built upon natural actions. Interactions through tangible and gesture-based systems allow a user to operate systems through intuitive actions based on natural human experience and behavior (O'Brien and Toms, 2008). To discover and understand how to control these types of systems, users may prefer to interact with a system using natural channels of communication with gestures that they are familiar with in everyday life, particularly those that are used to communicate with people. Gestures can take many forms, from simply using a hand to target something on the screen to specific continuous movement using the whole body for embodied interaction (Delamare et al., 2015). Dourish (2004) describes an approach to embodiment grounded in phenomenology that takes into account the fact that any understanding we have of the world is due to some initial physical exploration. When users approach an embodied interactive system, they must construct a new understanding of how it works on the basis of their physical exploration. Even though different people who approach a system may have the same starting point with direct experience itself, their expectations and prior experience will affect the way in which they initially explore the system and ultimately the mental model they construct of how the system works. Laptop and touchscreen interaction are ubiquitous enough that there are established guidelines and design patterns that designers adhere to (Norman, 1983). These patterns and guidelines cause users to have certain expectations of how a system might work even before they begin interacting with it. However, embodied interaction is relatively new and does not have as coherent a set of consistent design patterns for interaction. Therefore, designers and researchers need to carefully consider embodied cognition to understand embodied movement in defining a set of gestures for interactive systems. The cognitive methods that have emerged to facilitate designing the physical embodied actions for user input include: gesture-elicitation studies, body storming, metaphorical design, and protocol analysis. As we see more embodied interactive systems in the world, we will begin to see standards and consistent interaction models across the designs, and a new set of guidelines will emerge.

6.1.2   DESIGNING GESTURES WITH EFFECTIVE VISUAL FEEDBACK

Currently, designers create a context for understanding embodied gestures that relate to visual experience (Karam and Schraefel, 2005). In order to design gestures that are learnable within the context of embodied interactive systems, visual cues and feedback are essential components of the design. According to Norman (1983), gesture interfaces still have many problems, such as the difficulty of remembering which gestures to use and the lack of visual feedback. Designers need to carefully consider how to design interactive user experiences that engage and captivate the user by providing effective visual feedback. Because users expect to see increasing interactive functionality in displays, gesture design for gesture input methods relies on real-time visual feedback (Fagerberg et al., 2003). In order to create successful embodied interaction, embodied interaction can be designed to rely on the same movements we perform with our bodies and environment in our daily lives so that we re-use existing skills. By providing visual interaction feedback, interactive displays can become more effective at alerting users and inducing them to explore their interactive capabilities. The creation of visual feedback and designing of the gestures for interaction in gesture-based systems are challenging because little research to date has focused on standards for interaction feedback. Thoughtfully incorporating affordances and metaphors within the design process is critical to this challenge. The modalities for feedback can take different forms, including visual, audio, tactile, haptics/force, and smell. Embodied interaction challenges designers to explore alternative modalities to improve communication from the system to the user by confirming the current states and intentions of the user during interaction (Zhang et al., 2016).

6.1.3   UNDERSTANDING SENSING TECHNOLOGY

Since sensing technology is required to implement embodied interaction, designers need to understand the capabilities and limitations of alternative sensing technologies. Gesture recognition is an open research field that will impact the scope of possible gestures and tangible interaction that can be effectively incorporated into the design. As new sensing technologies are introduced to the design community, the design space for embodied interaction will expand. Recent sensor technologies for gesture recognition include the Nintendo WiiMote, the Microsoft Kinect, and the Leap Motion Controller; each with its own set of capabilities and limitations in the types of gestures and the part of the body it can sense. As the technologies that designers can integrate into their embodied interactive system expand, interaction designers need to consider issues of accuracy and fatigue. Successful embodied interaction design should take advantage of new technologies while maintaining simple and easy-to-perform gestures for interaction. An important consideration for the challenge of designing with relatively new sensing technology is to anticipate the balance and importance of epistemic vs. pragmatic actions in the user experience, and their potential to produce cognitive advantages and physical fatigue.

6.2 RESEARCH CHALLENGES FOR EMBODIED INTERCTION

6.2.1 GESTURE DESIGN

Research related to gesture design is relatively new, as is the concept of designing gestures. Unlike the research on gestures seen in human-to-human communication, the research on gesture design for use in embodied interaction has a relatively short history. Before the 1980s, a primary concern in gestural interaction research was poor usability (Bhuiyan and Picking, 2009). As affordable novel sensing technology emerged, the primary concern in gesture interaction research is the lack of a widely accepted definition and classification of gestures and the conventions or guidelines for the design of intuitive and natural embodied interaction. A research challenge is to identify the categories and specific implementations of gestures that create more effective embodied interactive systems. Recently, various applications with embodied interaction are emerging; however, they do not take into consideration the cognitive issues of embodiment, affordances, and learnability. Adaptation of existing and development of new design methods and experimental studies are critical research challenges for the design of gestures that people are expected to learn and use in embodied interactive systems.

There are numerous perspectives and considerations for the optimal design of embodied interaction. Horn (2013) proposes that the designer should think about cultural forms: social constructions or conventions associated with gestures, objects, and situations affects the user's existing cognitive, physical, and emotional resources. In addition, social acceptability is an important part of designing usable gestures for embodied interaction. Using gestures to interact with a public digital system may sometimes expect the use of socially or culturally embarrassing or disruptive gestures. We should not overlook the fact that the user perceives and pays attention to his/her situation, which is an important deciding factor for the user when interacting with the system (Rico and Brewster, 2009). Therefore, especially if the interaction conducted is performed in public places, more attention should be paid to social and cultural conventions when designing gestures.

6.2.2 MULTIDISCIPLINARY RESEARCH

Designing embodied interaction is a multidisciplinary topic requiring communication between the design community, technology developers, and cognitive science communities. Through collaboration and communication, researchers and designers are able to exchange ideas, and research perspectives, and apply the knowledge gained in one discipline to another discipline as a way to improve the gestural user interfaces. For example, technologists often focus on how sensing technologies can be employed to detect a user's presence and recognize various types of physical body input, and technology research communities usually overlook usefulness, usability, and applicability to human experience (Kuhlman, 2009). However, it is important to consider cognitive and physical issues to understand how gestures can communicate with the system in a way that reduces confusion, fatigue, or cognitive dissonance on the part of the user. The importance of interdisciplinary exchanges is recognized, but it is hindered by a lack of common goals, methods, and language. A significant research challenge for tangible and gesture-based interaction design is a better understanding of the research challenges in different disciplines and how these can impact a common goal of more effective interaction design.

6.2.3 FINDING APPROPRIATE CONTEXTS OF USE

Application areas for embodied interaction are diverse. Many projects are aimed at supporting learning and education. For example, tangible interaction can be used to enhance creativity, interactive music installations or instruments, museum installations, and tools to support planning and decision making. While there is good evidence that tangibles tend to support spatial cognition, it is, for example, less clear what kinds of tangibles, design knowledge, and guidelines are most effective in supporting spatial cognition. However, most systems have been designed and used in the lab as a research project. Research is needed to identify the context of use that takes advantage of embodied interaction systems and for which contexts and application areas they are the most suitable.

6.2.4 LIMITED SCOPE OF REPRESENTATION

Embodied interaction is embedded in physical space, and interaction therefore occurs by movement in physical space. Users interact directly with physical objects and experience their physicality, move around in their environment, and move objects around, trying to configure their environment according to their needs (Hornecker and Buur, 2006). The primary research issue is the link between the fundamental qualities of physicality and the spatial configuration of objects (Reeves, 2006). The use of physical objects has limitations of interactive surfaces, inflexibility, and difficulty in supporting complex commands because of a high degree of direct manipulation (Patten and Ishii, 2007). In this research topic, the advantage of the physicality of embodied interaction is considered a disadvantage: physical objects have a fixed geometry and specific purpose, where digital objects as interactive levers can adapt to the needs of the user. This can limit the versatility of embodied interactive systems.

6.2.5   COGNITIVE AND PHYSICAL FATIGUE

Prolonged use of gestures might cause some ergonomic issues, including physical discomfort and fatigue. Because embodied interaction uses physical forms, issues such as ergonomics and long-term strain have to be considered (Shaer and Hornecker, 2010; Toole, 2012). Ergonomic issues have to be considered not only for tangible interaction, but also gesture-based interaction. User fatigue is a common criticism of gestural interface, resulting from the need to move in unfamiliar ways to perform even simple interactions. Hence, designers must also apply an understanding of kinesiology and physiology in the ergonomics of human gesture to avoid hyperextension, repetition, and static positioning while utilizing relaxed, natural positions to prevent fatigue and injury during device use.

Bibliography

Abdelmohsen, S. M. and Do, E. Y. L. (2007). TangiCAD: Tangible Interface for Manipulating Architectural 3D Models. In *the10th International Conference on Computer Aided Architectural Design Research in Asia (CAADRIA)*. Nanjing, China. 16

Ackad, C., Kay, J., and Tomitsch, M. (2014). Toward learnable gestures for exploring hierarchical information spaces at a large public display. In *CHI'14 Workshop on Gesture-based Interaction Design*. 49, 57

Aimaiti, N. and Yan, X. (2011). Gesture-based Interaction and Implication for the Future. Master's Thesis. Umea University. 56

Alt, F., Schmidt, A., and Müller, J. (2012). Advertising on public display networks. *Computer*, 45(5), 50–56. DOI: 10.1109/MC.2012.150. 58

Anderson, D., Frankel, J. L., Marks, J., Agarwala, A., Beardsley, P., Hodgins, J., Leigh, D., Ryall, K., Sullivan, E., and Yedidia, J. S. (2000, July). Tangible interaction+ graphical interpretation: a new approach to 3D modeling. In *Proceedings of the 27th Annual Conference on Computer Graphics and Interactive Techniques* (pp. 393–402). ACM Press/Addison-Wesley Publishing Co. DOI: 10.1145/344779.344960. 16

Antle, A. N., Corness, G., and Droumeva, M. (2009). Human-computer-intuition? Exploring the cognitive basis for intuition in embodied interaction. *International Journal of Arts and Technology*, 2(3), 235–254. DOI: 10.1504/IJART.2009.028927. 1

Antle, A. N., Marshall, P., and van den Hoven, E. (2011). Embodied interaction: Theory and practice in HCI. In *Proc. CHI* (Vol. 11). DOI: 10.1145/1979742.1979592. 1, 2

ArchiCAD: http://www.graphisoft.com/archicad/.

ARToolKit: https://artoolkit.org/.

Baber, C. (2014). Objects as Agents: how ergotic and epistemic gestures could benefit gesture-based interaction. Gesture-based interaction Design: Communication and Cognition, *CHI 2014 Workshop*. 57

Bakker, S., Antle, A. N., and Van Den Hoven, E. (2012). Embodied metaphors in tangible interaction design. *Personal and Ubiquitous Computing*, 16(4), 433–449. DOI: 10.1007/s00779-011-0410-4. 5, 16

Bhuiyan, M. and Picking, R. (2009, November). Gesture-controlled user interfaces, what have we done and what's next. In *Proceedings of the Fifth Collaborative Research Symposium on Security, E-Learning, Internet and Networking (SEIN 2009)*, (pp. 25–29), Darmstadt, Germany. 93

Billinghurst, M., Kato, H., and Poupyrev, I. (2001). The MagicBook: a transitional AR interface. *Computers & Graphics*, 25(5), 745–753. DOI: 10.1016/S0097-8493(01)00117-0.

Boren, T. and Ramey, J. (2000). Thinking aloud: Reconciling theory and practice. *IEEE Transactions on Professional Communication* 43.3 261–278. DOI: 10.1109/47.867942. 31, 71

Brereton, M. and McGarry, B. (2000, April). An observational study of how objects support engineering design thinking and communication: implications for the design of tangible media. In *Proceedings of the SIGCHI conference on Human Factors in Computing Systems* (pp. 217–224). ACM. DOI: 10.1145/332040.332434. 4

Burlamaqui, L. and Dong, A. (2015). The use and misuse of the concept of affordance. In *Design Computing and Cognition'14* (pp. 295–311). Springer International Publishing. DOI: 10.1007/978-3-319-14956-1_17. 4

Cabreira, A. T. and Hwang, F. (2015). An analysis of mid-air gestures used across three platforms. In *Proceedings of the 2015 British HCI Conference*, (pp. 257–258). ACM. DOI: 10.1145/2783446.2783599. 49

Card, S. K. (2014). A simple universal gesture scheme for user interfaces. Gesture-based interaction Design: Communication and Cognition, *CHI 2014 Workshop*. 57

Cartmill, E. A., Beilock, S., and Goldin-Meadow, S. (2012). A word in the hand: action, gesture and mental representation in humans and non-human primates. *Phil. Trans. R. Soc. B*, 367(1585), 129–143. DOI: 10.1098/rstb.2011.0162. 57

Chen, I. M., Xing, S., Tay, R., and Yeo, S. H. (2005). Many strings attached: from conventional to robotic marionette manipulation. *Robotics and Automation Magazine*, IEEE, 59–74. DOI: 10.1109/MRA.2005.1411420. 79

Cook, S. W., Mitchell, Z., and Goldin-Meadow, S. (2008). Gesturing makes learning last. *Cognition*. 106(2), 1047–1058. DOI: 10.1016/j.cognition.2007.04.010. 2

Dan, R. B. and Mohod, P. S. (2014). Survey on Hand Gesture Recognition Approaches. *International Journal of Computer Science and Information Technologies*, 5 (2), 2050–2052. 2

Delamare, W., Coutrix, C., and Nigay, L. (2015). Designing guiding systems for gesture-based interaction. In *Proceedings of the 7th ACM SIGCHI Symposium on Engineering Interactive Computing Systems*. ACM. 44–53. DOI: 10.1145/2774225.2774847. 49, 91

Dillon, A. (2003). User interface design. *MacMillan Encyclopedia of Cognitive Science*, London: MacMillan, (4) 453–458. 1, 2, 5

Dourish, P. (2001). Seeking a foundation for context-aware computing. *Human–Computer Interaction*, 16(2–4), 229–241. DOI: 10.1207/S15327051HCI16234_07. 2

Dourish, P. (2004). *Where the Action Is: The Foundations of Embodied Interaction*. MIT Press. 1, 3, 91

Efron, D. (1941). *Gesture and Environment*. King's Crown Press. 2

Egerstedt, M., Murphey, T., and Ludwig, J. (2007, April). Motion programs for puppet choreography and control. In *International Workshop on Hybrid Systems: Computation and Control* (pp. 190–202). Springer Berlin Heidelberg. DOI: 10.1007/978-3-540-71493-4_17. 57

Fagerberg, P., Ståhl, A., and Höök, K. (2003). Designing gestures for affective input: an analysis of shape, effort and valence. ACM. 92

Fishkin, K. P. (2004). A taxonomy for and analysis of tangible interfaces. *Personal and Ubiquitous Computing*, 8(5), 347–358. DOI: 10.1007/s00779-004-0297-4. 5, 7, 10

Fitzmaurice, G. W. (1996). Graspable user interfaces (Doctoral dissertation, University of Toronto). 4, 5, 7, 10, 12, 13, 14

Fitzmaurice, G. W. and Buxton, W. (1997, March). An empirical evaluation of graspable user interfaces: toward specialized, space-multiplexed input. In *Proceedings of the ACM SIGCHI Conference on Human Factors in Computing Systems* (pp. 43–50). ACM. DOI: 10.1145/258549.258578. 4, 10, 11

Fjeld, M., Bichsel, M., and Rauterberg, M. (1997, September). BUILD-IT: an intuitive design tool based on direct object manipulation. In *International Gesture Workshop* (pp. 297–308). Springer Berlin Heidelberg. 17, 19

Foreman, N. and Gillett, R. (1997). *A Handbook of Spatial Research Paradigms and Methodologies* (Vol. 2). Psychology Press. 40

Gero, J. S. and Tang, H. H. (2001). The differences between retrospective and concurrent protocols in revealing the process-oriented aspects of the design process. *Design Studies*, 22(3), 283–295. DOI: 10.1016/S0142-694X(00)00030-2. 40

Gibson, E. J. (1982). The concept of affordances in development: The renascence of functionalism. In *The concept of development: The Minnesota symposia on child psychology* (Vol. 15, pp. 55–81). Lawrence Erlbaum Hillsdale, NJ. 4

Goldin-Meadow S. and Beilock S. L. (2010). Action's influence on thought: The case of gesture. *Perspectives on Psychological Science*, 5(6): 664–674. DOI: 10.1177/1745691610388764. 3, 49

Goldin-Meadow, S. (1999). The role of gesture in communication and thinking. *Trends in Cognitive Sciences*, 3(11), 419–429. DOI: 10.1016/S1364-6613(99)01397-2. 49

Goldin-Meadow, S. (2006). Talking and thinking with our hands. *Current Directions in Psychological Science*, 15(1), 34–39. DOI: 10.1111/j.0963-7214.2006.00402.x.

Grace, K., Wasinger, R., Ackad, C., Collins, A., Dawson, O., Gluga, R., Kay, J., and Tomitsch, M. (2013). Conveying interactivity at an interactive public information display. In *Proceedings of the 2nd ACM International Symposium on Pervasive Displays*, (pp. 19–24). ACM. DOI: 10.1145/2491568.2491573. 58, 63

Hanington, B. and Martin, B. (2012). *Universal Methods of Design: 100 Ways to Research Complex Problems, Develop Innovative Ideas, and Design Effective Solutions*. Rockport Publishers. 21

Hinrichs, U., Carpendale, S., Valkanova, N., Kuikkaniemi, K., Jacucci, G., and Vande Moere, A. (2013). Interactive public displays. *Computer Graphics and Applications*, IEEE, 33(2), 25–27. DOI: 10.1109/MCG.2013.28. 49, 52

Hoffmann, G. (1996). Teach-in of a robot by showing the motion. In *Proceedings of Image Processing*, (pp. 529–532). IEEE. DOI: 10.1109/icip.1996.559550. 54

Horn, M. S. (2013, February). The role of cultural forms in tangible interaction design. In *Proceedings of the 7th International Conference on Tangible, Embedded and Embodied Interaction* (pp. 117–124). ACM. DOI: 10.1145/2460625.2460643. 93

Hornecker, E. (2005). A design theme for tangible interaction: embodied facilitation. In *ECSCW 2005*. Springer Netherlands. 23–43. DOI: 10.1007/1-4020-4023-7_2. 13

Hornecker, E. and Buur, J. (2006). Getting a grip on tangible interaction: a framework on physical space and social interaction. In *Proceedings of the SIGCHI Conference on Human Factors in Computing Systems*, (pp. 437–446). ACM. DOI: 10.1145/1124772.1124838. 16, 94

Ishii, H. and Ullmer B (1997). Tangible bits: toward seamless interfaces between people, bits, and atoms. In *Proceedings of the CHI'97 Conference on Human Factors in Computing Systems*, (pp. 234–241). Atlanta, Georgia, March. DOI: 10.1145/258549.258715. 4, 7

Jacko, J. A. (Ed.). (2012). *Human Computer Interaction Handbook: Fundamentals, Evolving Technologies, and Emerging Applications*. CRC Press. 11

Jenkins, O. C., González, G. and Loper, M. M. (2007), Tracking human motion and actions for interactive robots. In *Proceedings of the ACM/IEEE International Conference on Human-robot Interaction*, (pp. 365–372). ACM. DOI: 10.1145/1228716.1228765. 54

Jetter, H. C. (2014). A Cognitive Perspective on Gestures, Manipulations, and Space in Future Multi-Device Interaction. In *Proceedings of CHI Workshop on Gesture-based Interaction Design: Communication and Cognition*, Toronto, Canada. 49, 57

Karam, M. and Schraefel, M.C. (2005). A Taxonomy of Gestures in Human Computer Interactions. Technical report. University of Southampton. 57, 92

Kato, H., Billinghurst, M., and Poupyrev, I. (2000). Virtual object manipulation on a table-top AR environment. In Proceedings of the IEEE and ACM International Symposium on Augmented Reality. IEEE. DOI: 10.1109/ISAR.2000.880934. 14, 17

Kaushik, D. and Jain, R. (2014). Natural user interfaces: trend in virtual interaction. arXiv preprint arXiv:1405.0101. *International Journal Of Latest Technology in Engineering, Management & Applied Science* (IJLTEMAS) 3(4), 141–143. 56

Kessell A. and Tversky B (2006). Using diagrams and gestures to think and talk about insight problems. In *Proceedings of the Meeting of the Cognitive Science Society*, (pp. 2528–2537). 2, 3

Kim, M. J. and Maher, M. L. (2007). The effects of tangible user interfaces on designers' spatial cognition. Key Centre of Design Computing and Cognition, Faculty of Architecture, University of Sydney. 5, 42, 43, 44

Kim, M. J. and Maher, M. L. (2008). The impact of tangible user interfaces on spatial cognition during collaborative design. *Design Studies*, 29(3), 222–253. DOI: 10.1016/j.destud.2007.12.006. 9, 12, 40, 41

Kirsh, D. and Maglio, P. (1994). On distinguishing epistemic from pragmatic action. *CognitiveScience*, 18(4), 513–549. DOI: 10.1207/s15516709cog1804_1. 5

Klemmer, S. R., Hartmann, B., and Takayama, L. (2006). How bodies matter: five themes for interaction design. In *Proceedings of the 6th conference on Designing Interactive Systems* (pp. 140–149). ACM. DOI: 10.1145/1142405.1142429. 1

Kuhlman, L. M. (2009). Gesture mapping for interaction design: an investigative process for developing interactive gesture libraries (Doctoral dissertation, The Ohio State University). 94

Le Goc, M., Dragicevic, P., Huron, S., Boy, J. and Fekete, J. D. (2015). SmartTokens: Embedding motion and grip sensing in small tangible objects. In *Proceedings of the 28th Annual ACM Symposium on User Interface Software & Technology*, (pp. 357–362). ACM. DOI: 10.1145/2807442.2807488. 12

Lederman, S. J. and Klatzky, R. L. (1993). Extracting object properties through haptic exploration. *Acta Psychologica*, 84(1), 29–40. DOI: 10.1016/0001-6918(93)90070-8. 4

Lee, L., Javed, Y., Danilowicz, S., and Maher, M. L. (2014). Information at the wave of your hand. In *Proceedings of HCI Korea*, (pp. 63–70). Hanbit Media, Inc. 49

Leganchuk, A., Zhai, S., and Buxton, W. (1998). Manual and cognitive benefits of two-handed input: an experimental study. *ACM Transactions on Computer-Human Interaction* (TOCHI), 5(4), 326–359. DOI: 10.1145/300520.300522. 4

Leigh, S. W., Schoessler, P., Heibeck, F., Maes, P., and Ishii, H. (2015). THAW: tangible interaction with see-through augmentation for smartphones on computer screens. In *Proceedings of the Ninth International Conference on Tangible, Embedded, and Embodied Interaction*, *(pp. 89–96). ACM. DOI: 10.1145/2677199.2680584. 16

Li, W., Zhang, Z., and Liu, Z. (2008). Expandable data-driven graphical modeling of human actions based on salient postures. *Circuits and Systems for Video Technology*, (pp. 1499–1510). IEEE. DOI: 10.1109/TCSVT.2008.2005597. 54

Li, W., Zhang, Z., and Liu, Z. (2010) Action recognition based on a bag of 3d points. In *Computer Vision and Pattern Recognition Workshops (CVPRW)*, (pp. 9–14). IEEE. DOI: 10.1109/cvprw.2010.5543273. 54

Liu, G., Zhang, J., Wang, W., and McMillan, L. (2005). A system for analyzing and indexing human-motion databases. In *Proceedings of the 2005 ACM SIGMOD International Conference on Management of Data*, (pp. 924–926). ACM. DOI: 10.1145/1066157.1066290. 54

Liu, K., Kaleas, D., and Ruuspakka, R. (2012). Prototyping interaction with everyday artifacts: training and recognizing 3D objects via Kinects. In *Proceedings of the Sixth International Conference on Tangible, Embedded and Embodied Interaction*, (pp. 241–244). ACM. DOI: 10.1145/2148131.2148182. 54

Loomis, J. M. and Lederman, S. J. (1986). Tactual perception. *Handbook of Perception and Human Performances*, 2, 2. 4

Magerkurth, C. and Peter, T. (2002). Augmenting tabletop design for computer-supported cooperative work. In *Workshop on Co-located Tabletop Collaboration: Technologies and Directions at CSCW* (Vol. 2, p. 2002). 12

Maher, M. L., Gero, J., Lee, L., Yu, R., and Clausner, T. (2016). Measuring the effect of tangible interaction on design cognition. In *Proceedings, Part I, 10th International Conference on Foundations of Augmented Cognition: Neuroergonomics and Operational Neuroscience*. Vol. 9743 (pp. 348–360). Springer-Verlag:New York, Inc. DOI: 10.1007/978-3-319-39955-3_33. 24

Maher, M. L., Clausner, T.C., Gonzalez, B., and Grace, K. (2014). Gesture in the Crossroads of HCI and Creative Cognition. Gesture-based interaction Design: Communication and Cognition, *CHI 2014 Workshop*. 19. 57

Maher, M. L. and Kim, M. J. (2005, September). Do tangible user interfaces impact spatial cognition in collaborative design?. In *International Conference on Cooperative Design, Visualization and Engineering* (pp. 30–41). Springer Berlin Heidelberg. DOI: 10.1007/11555223_4. 12

Mahzoon, M., Maher, M. L., Grace, K., LoCurto, L., and Outcault, B. (2016, July). *The willful marionette*: Modeling social cognition using gesture-gesture interaction dialogue. In *International Conference on Augmented Cognition* (pp. 402–413). Springer International Publishing. DOI: 10.1007/978-3-319-39952-2_39. 79

Martin, B., Hanington, B., and Hanington, B. M. (2012). *Universal Methods of Design: 100 Ways to Research Complex Problems, Develop Innovative Ideas, and Design Effective Solutions*. Rockport Publishers. 62

McNeill, D. (1992). *Hand and Mind: What Gestures Reveal about Thought*. University of Chicago Press. 2, 49

McNeill, D. (2008). *Gesture and Thought*. University of Chicago Press. 2

Memarovic, N., Langheinrich, M., Alt, F., Elhart, I., Hosio, S., and Rubegni, E. (2012). Using public displays to stimulate passive engagement, active engagement, and discovery in public spaces. In *Proceedings of the 4th Media Architecture Biennale Conference: Participation*, (pp. 55–64). ACM. DOI: 10.1145/2421076.2421086. 58

Merrill, D., Sun, E., and Kalanithi, J. (2012). Sifteo cubes™. In *CHI'12 Extended Abstracts on Human Factors in Computing Systems*, *(pp.* 1015–1018). ACM. DOI: 10.1145/2212776.2212374. 9

Michelis, D. and Müller, J. (2011). The audience funnel: Observations of gesture based interaction with multiple large displays in a city center. *International Journal of Human–Computer Interaction*, 27(6), 562–579. DOI: 10.1080/10447318.2011.555299. 55

Mohnkern, K. E. (1997). Affordances, Metaphor, and Interface Design (Doctoral dissertation, Carnegie Mellon University). 5

Morris, M. R. (2012). Web on the wall: insights from a multimodal interaction elicitation study. In *Proceedings of the 2012 ACM International Conference on Interactive Tabletops and Surfaces*, (pp. 95–104). ACM. DOI: 10.1145/2396636.2396651. 63, 70

Motta, T. and Nedel, L. (2013). Interactive public displays: A gesture-based proposal using Kinect. *SBC Journal on Interactive Systems*, 4(2), 43–54. 52

Mullaney, T., Yttergren, B., and Stolterman, E. (2014). Positional acts: using a Kinect™ sensor to reconfigure patient roles within radiotherapy treatment. In *Proceedings of the 8th International Conference on Tangible, Embedded and Embodied Interaction*, (pp. 93–96). ACM, DOI: 10.1145/2540930.2540943. 54

Müller, J., Alt, F., Michelis, D., and Schmidt, A. (2010). Requirements and design space for interactive public displays. In *Proceedings of the International Conference on Multimedia*, (pp. 1285–1294). ACM. DOI: 10.1145/1873951.1874203. 49, 58

Murphey, T. D. and Egerstedt, M. B. (2008). Choreography for Marionettes: Imitation, Planning, and Control. In *Proc. of IEEE Int. Conf. on Intelligent and Robotic (IROS) Workshop on Art and Robotics*. 57

Murphey, T. D. and Johnson, E. R. (2011). Control aesthetics in software architecture for robotic marionettes. In *American Control Conference (ACC)*, (pp. 3825–3830). IEEE. DOI: 10.1109/acc.2011.5991246. 57

Namy, L. L. and Newcombe, N. S. (2008). More than just hand waving: review of hearing gestures: how our hands help us think. *Journal of Cognition and Development*, 9(2), 247–252. Chicago Press. DOI: 10.1080/15248370802022753. 49

New Kinect Example Average Point Tracking, http://shiffman.net/2011/01/13/new-kinect-example-average-point-tracking/.

Nielsen, J. and Molich, R. (1990). Heuristic evaluation of user interfaces. In *Proceedings of the SIGCHI Conference on Human Factors in Computing Systems: Empowering People*, (pp. 249–256). ACM. DOI: 10.1145/97243.97281. 28

Nielsen, J. (1994). Heuristic evaluation. In: Nielsen, J., Mack, R.L. (Eds.), *Usability Inspection Methods*, Wiley, New York. 28, 64, 75, 77

Nielsen, M., Störring, M., Moeslund, T. B., and Granum, E. (2003). A procedure for developing intuitive and ergonomic gesture interfaces for man-machine interaction. In *Proceedings of the 5th International Gesture Workshop*. Springer-Verlag Berlin Heidelberg, pp. 409–420. DOI: 10.1007/978-3-540-24598-8_38. 17, 61

Norman, D. A. (1983). Some observations on mental models. *Mental Models*, 7(112), 7–14. 1, 91, 92

Norman, D. A. (1988). *The Psychology of Everyday Things*. Basic Books. 3

Norman, D. A. (2002). Emotion & design: attractive things work better. *Interactions*, 9(4), 36–42. DOI: 10.1145/543434.543435. 64

Norman, D. A. (2005). *Emotional Design: Why We Love (or Hate) Everyday Things*. Basic Books. 28, 60

O'Brien, H. L. and Toms, E. G. (2008). What is user engagement? A conceptual framework for defining user engagement with technology. *Journal of the American Society for Information Science and Technology*, 59(6), 938–955. DOI: 10.1002/asi.20801. 58, 91

Osmo: https://www.playosmo.com/en/.

Oviatt, S. (2006). Human-centered design meets cognitive load theory: designing interfaces that help people think. In *Proceedings of the 14th annual ACM International Conference on Multimedia, (pp.* 871–880). ACM. DOI: 10.1145/1180639.1180831. 49

Patten, J. and Ishii, H. (2007). Mechanical constraints as computational constraints in tabletop tangible interfaces. In *Proceedings of the SIGCHI Conference on Human Factors in Computing Systems*, (pp. 809–818). ACM. DOI: 10.1145/1240624.1240746. 11, 94

Petridis, P., Mania, K., Pletinckx, D., and White, M. (2006, November). Usability evaluation of the epoch multimodal user interface: designing 3d tangible interactions. In *Proceedings of the ACM Symposium on Virtual Reality Software and Technology* (pp. 116–122). ACM. DOI: 10.1145/1180495.1180521. 7

Pollard, N. S., Hodgins, J. K., Riley, M. J. and Atkeson, C. G. (2002) Adapting human motion for the control of a humanoid robot. In *Robotics and Automation ICRA'02*, (pp. 1390–1397). IEEE. DOI: 10.1109/robot.2002.1014737. 54

Pyryeskin, D., Hancock, M., and Hoey, J. (2012). Comparing elicited gestures to designer-created gestures for selection above a multitouch surface. In *Proceedings of the 2012 ACM International Conference on Interactive Tabletops and Surfaces*, (pp. 1–10). ACM. DOI: 10.1145/2396636.2396638. 61

Raptis, M., Kirovski, D., and Hoppe, H. (2011). Real-time classification of dance gestures from skeleton animation. In *Proceedings of the 2011 ACM SIGGRAPH/Eurographics Symposium on Computer Animation*, (pp. 147–156). ACM. DOI: 10.1145/2019406.2019426. 54

Reeves, S. (2006, February). Physicality, spatial configuration and computational objects. In *First International Workshop on Physicality*. 94

Rico, J. and Brewster, S. (2009, September). Gestures all around us: user differences in social acceptability perceptions of gesture based interfaces. In *Proceedings of the 11th International Conference on Human-Computer Interaction with Mobile Devices and Services* (p. 64). ACM. DOI: 10.1145/1613858.1613936. 93

Rico, J., Crossan, A., and Brewster, S. (2011). Gesture-based interfaces: Practical applications of gestures in real world mobile settings. In *Whole Body Interaction*, (pp. 173–186). Springer London. DOI: 10.1007/978-0-85729-433-3_14. 49

Robert, D., Wistorrt, R., Gray, J. and Breazeal, C. (2011). Exploring mixed reality robot gaming. In *Proceedings of the Fifth International Conference on Tangible, Embedded, and Embodied Interaction*, (pp. 125–128). ACM. DOI: 10.1145/1935701.1935726. 79

Saffer, D. (2008). *Designing Gestural Interfaces: Touchscreens and Interactive Devices*. O'Reilly Media, Inc. 49

Saunders, R. and Gero, J. S. (2004). Curious agents and situated design evaluations. *AI EDAM: Artificial Intelligence for Engineering Design, Analysis and Manufacturing*, 18(02), 153–161. DOI: 10.1017/s0890060404040119.

Schmidt, V. A. (2010). User interface design patterns. Air Force Research Lab Wright-Patterson Afb Oh Human Effectiveness Directorate. 21

Schönböck, J., König, F., Kotsis, G., Gruber, D., Zaim, E., and Schmidt, A. (2008). MirrorBoard – An Interactive Billboard. In *Proceedings of Mensch und Computer* 2008. Oldenbourg Verlag Lübeck, 207–216. 59

Sclaroff, S., Betke, M., Kollios, G., Alon, J., Athitsos, V., Li, R., and Tian, T. P. (2005). Tracking, analysis, and recognition of human gestures in video. In *Eighth International Conference on Document Analysis and Recognition (ICDAR'05), (pp.* 806–810). IEEE. DOI: 10.1109/ICDAR.2005.243. 49

Segal, A. (2011). Do gestural interfaces promote thinking? Embodied interaction: Congruent gestures and direct touch promote performance in math (Doctoral dissertation, Columbia University).

Seyed, T., Burns, C., Costa Sousa, M., Maurer, F., and Tang, A. (2012). Eliciting usable gestures for multi-display environments. In *Proceedings of the 2012 ACM International Conference on Interactive Tabletops and Surfaces*, (pp. 41–50). ACM. DOI: 10.1145/2396636.2396643. 57, 67

Shaer, O. Z. (2008). A visual language for specifying and programming tangible user interfaces. ProQuest. 7

Shaer, O. and Hornecker, E. (2010). Tangible user interfaces: past, present, and future directions.*Foundations and Trends in Human-Computer Interaction*, 3(1–2), 1-137. DOI: 10.1561/1100000026. 7, 10, 11, 15, 16, 95

Shaer, O. and Jacob, R. J. (2009). A specification paradigm for the design and implementation of tangible user interfaces. *ACM Transactions on Computer-Human Interaction (TOCHI)*, 16(4), 20. DOI: 10.1145/1614390.1614395. 7, 15, 16, 17, 19

Shaer, O., Leland, N., Calvillo-Gamez, E. H., and Jacob, R. J. K. (2004). The tac paradigm: Specifying tangible user interfaces. *Personal and Ubiquitous Computing* 8, 5, 359–369. DOI: 10.1007/s00779-004-0298-3. 15

Sharp, H. (2003). *Interaction Design.* John Wiley & Sons. 21

Sidner, C. L., Lee, C., Kidd, C. D., Lesh, N., and Rich, C. (2005). Explorations in engagement for humans and robots. *Artificial Intelligence*, 140–164. DOI: 10.1016/j.artint.2005.03.005. 79

Song, Y., Demirdjian, D., and Davis, R. (2011). Tracking body and hands for gesture recognition: Natops aircraft handling signals database. In *Automatic Face & Gesture Recognition and Workshops (FG 2011), 2011 IEEE International Conference on*, (pp. 500–506). IEEE. DOI: 10.1109/FG.2011.5771448. 49

Speed, C., Pschetz, L., Oberlander, J. and Papadopoulos-Korfiatis, A. (2014). Dancing robots. In *Proceedings of the 8th International Conference on Tangible, Embedded and Embodied Interaction*, (pp. 353–356). ACM. DOI: 10.1145/2540930.2567898. 79

Sung, J., Ponce, C., Selman, B., and Saxena, A. (2012). Unstructured human activity detection from rgbd images. In *Robotics and Automation (ICRA)*, (pp. 842–849). IEEE. DOI: 10.1109/ICRA.2012.6224591. 54

Szabó, K. (1995). Metaphors and the user interface. URL: http://www.katalinszabo.com/metaphor.htm (visited on 03/05/2015). 5

Tang, M. (2011). Recognizing hand gestures with microsoft's kinect. Palo Alto: Department of Electrical Engineering of Stanford University. 54

Toole Jr., C. (2012). Software Architectural Support for Tangible User Interfaces in Distributed, Heterogeneous Computing Environments (Doctoral dissertation, Jackson State University). 95

Triesch, J., and Von Der Malsburg, C. (1998). *A Gesture Interface for Human-Robot-Interaction*. 98, 14–16. DOI: 10.1109/afgr.1998.671005. 54

Tversky, B., Jamalian, A., Segal, A., Giardino, V. and Kang, S.M. (2014). Congruent Gestures can Promote Thought. *Gesture-based interaction Design: Communication and Cognition, CHI 2014 Workshop.* 57

Ullmer, B. A. (1997). Models and mechanisms for tangible user interfaces (Masters Dissertation, Massachusetts Institute of Technology).

Ullmer, B. A. (2002). Tangible interfaces for manipulating aggregates of digital information (Doctoral Dissertation, Massachusetts Institute of Technology). 16

Ullmer, B. and Ishii, H. (1997). The metaDESK: models and prototypes for tangible user interfaces. In *Proceedings of the 10th Annual ACM Symposium on User Interface Software and Technology*, (pp. 223–232). ACM. DOI: 10.1145/263407.263551. 10

Ullmer, B. and Ishii, H. (2000). Emerging frameworks for tangible user interfaces. *IBM Systems Journal*, 39(3.4), 915–931. DOI: 10.1147/sj.393.0915. 7, 13

Valdes, C., Eastman, D., Grote, C., Thatte, S., Shaer, O., Mazalek, A., and Konkel, M. K. (2014). Exploring the design space of gestural interaction with active tokens through user-defined gestures. In *Proceedings of the SIGCHI Conference on Human Factors in Computing Systems*, (pp. 4107–4116). ACM. DOI: 10.1145/2556288.2557373. 13, 18

van den Hoven, E. and Mazalek, A. (2011). Grasping gestures: Gesturing with physical artifacts. *Artificial Intelligence for Engineering Design, Analysis and Manufacturing*, 25(03), 255–271. DOI: 10.1017/S0890060411000072. 5, 18

Vanacken, D. and Beznosyk, A. (2014). Help Systems for Gestural Interfaces and Their Effect on Collaboration and Communication. *Gesture-based interaction Design: Communication and Cognition, CHI 2014 Workshop.* 57

Viégas, F. B. and Wattenberg, M. (2007). Artistic data visualization: Beyond visual analytics. In *Online Communities and Social Computing*, (pp. 182–191). Springer. DOI: 10.1007/978-3-540-73257-0_21. 58

Waldherr, S., Romero, R., and Thrun, S. (2000). A gesture based interface for human-robot interaction. *Autonomous Robots*, 151–173. DOI: 10.1023/A:1008918401478. 54

Waldner, M., Hauber, J., Zauner, J., Haller, M., and Billinghurst, M. (2006). Tangible tiles: design and evaluation of a tangible user interface in a collaborative tabletop setup. In *Proceedings of the 18th Australia Conference on Computer-Human Interaction: Design: Activities, Artifacts and Environments*, (pp. 151–158). ACM. DOI: 10.1145/1228175.1228203. 13

Walter, R., Bailly, G., and Müller, J. (2013, April). StrikeAPose: revealing mid-air gestures on public displays. In *Proceedings of the SIGCHI Conference on Human Factors in Computing Systems* (pp. 841–850). ACM. DOI: 10.1145/2470654.2470774. 52, 53

Wang, Q., Li, C., Huang, X., and Tang, M. (2002). Tangible interface: integration of the real and virtual. In *Computer Supported Cooperative Work in Design, 2002. The 7th International Conference on* (pp. 408–412). IEEE. DOI: 10.1109/CSCWD.2002.1047723. 4

Want, R., Fishkin, K. P., Gujar, A., and Harrison, B. L. (1999, May). Bridging physical and virtual worlds with electronic tags. In *Proceedings of the SIGCHI Conference on Human Factors in Computing Systems* (pp. 370–377). ACM. DOI: 10.1145/302979.303111. 16

Wellner, P., Mackay, W., and Gold, R. (1993). Computer-augmented environments: back to the real world. *Communications of the ACM*, 36(7), 24–27. DOI: 10.1145/159544.159555. 16

Wobbrock, J. O., Aung, H. H., Rothrock, B., and Myers, B. (2005). A. Maximizing the guessability of symbolic input. In *CHI'05 Extended Abstracts on Human Factors in Computing Systems*, (pp. 1869–1872). ACM. DOI: 10.1145/1056808.1057043. 70

Wobbrock, J. O., Morris, M. R., and Wilson, A. D. (2009) User-defined gestures for surface computing. In *Proceedings of the SIGCHI Conference on Human Factors in Computing Systems*. (pp. 1083–1092). ACM. DOI: 10.1145/1518701.1518866. 70

Xu, J., Gannon, P. J., Emmorey, K., Smith, J. F., and Braun, A. R. (2009). Symbolic gestures and spoken language are processed by a common neural system. *Proceedings of the National Academy of Sciences*, 106(49), 20664–20669. DOI: 10.1073/pnas.0909197106. 18

Yamane, K., Hodgins, J. K. and Brown, H. B. (2004). Controlling a motorized marionette with human motion capture data. *International Journal of Humanoid Robotics*, 651–669. DOI: 10.1142/S0219843604000319. 54, 79

Yang, H. D., Park, A. Y. and Lee, S. W. (2007). Gesture spotting and recognition for human–robot interaction. *Robotics*, (pp. 256–270). IEEE. DOI: 10.1109/TRO.2006.889491. 54

Zhang, T., Li, Y. T., and Wachs, J. P. (2016). The Effect of Embodied Interaction in Visual-Spatial Navigation. *ACM Transactions on Interactive Intelligent Systems* (TiiS), 7(1), 3. DOI: 10.1145/2953887. 92

Zigelbaum, J., and Csikszentmihályi, C. (2007). Reflecting on tangible user interfaces: three issues concerning domestic technology. Cambridge: MIT Media Lab. 19

Authors' Biographies

Mary Lou Maher is Professor and Chair of Software and Information Systems at UNC Charlotte and Honorary Professor of Design Computing in the Design Lab at the University of Sydney. At UNC Charlotte, she has established a concentration in HCI in the B.A. in Computer Science and in the M.S. in Information Technology. She has established a Design Studio and a Maker Space in the Department of Software and Information Systems. While at the University of Sydney, she created a new undergraduate degree called a Bachelor of Design Computing. While a Program Director at NSF, she started a funding program called CreativeIT. Dr. Maher's research interests include: cognitive effects of embodied interaction modalities, computational and cognitive models of creativity, and design patterns for active learning strategies in CS education.

Lina Lee is a Ph.D. student in the College of Computing and Informatics at UNC Charlotte. She received a B.S. and a M.S. in Housing and Interior Design from Kyung Hee University in South Korea. After then, she received a dual degree: M.S. in Architecture and M.S. in Information Technology Software at UNC Charlotte. She is a member of the InDe Lab and HCI Lab at UNC Charlotte. Her research interest is in the area of Human-Computer Interaction with particular focus on designing an interactive information system with gesture-based interactive techniques that enhance public engagement with interactive systems.

Printed in the United States
by Baker & Taylor Publisher Services